Adolf Hitler

My Part in His Downfall

Also by **Spike Milligan**

SPIKE MILLIGAN

𝕬𝖉𝖔𝖑𝖋 𝕳𝖎𝖙𝖑𝖊𝖗

My Part in His Downfall

London

MICHAEL JOSEPH

First published in Great Britain by
MICHAEL JOSEPH LTD
52 Bedford Square
London, W.C.1
JUNE 1971
SECOND IMPRESSION JULY 1971
THIRD IMPRESSION JULY 1971
FOURTH IMPRESSION NOVEMBER 1971

7181 0886 3

Photoset in Great Britain by
Filmtype Services Limited, Scarborough,
Yorkshire
in ten on twelve point Century Medium
Printed by Hollen Street Press Ltd., Slough
on paper supplied by Book Papers Ltd.,
and bound by James Burn
at Esher, Surrey

I dedicate this book to
Norma Farnes,
my manager, who puts
up with me.

Contents

Acknowledgements

I am grateful to John Counsell for permission to quote from his book, COUNSELL'S OPINION; and to the Director of the Imperial War Museum for permission to reproduce three photographs in the Museum's possession.

Preface

This book is the first volume of a trilogy. It will cover the time of my joining the Artillery till the time we landed at Algiers. Volume II will cover from going into action till VJ day. Volume III will cover from my demob to my eventual return to England. All the salient facts are true, I have garnished some of them in my own manner, but the basic facts are, as I say, true. I have used the simple language of the barrack room and used the normal quota of swearing. Some of the revelations are very bawdy but these I have told exactly as they happened. It wasn't all fun, but as you will see, a lot of it was. The experience of being in the Army changed my whole life, I never believed that an organization such as ours could ever go to war, leave alone win it. It was, as Yeats remarked of the Easter Rising, 'A terrible beauty'. There were the deaths of some of my friends, and therefore, no matter how funny I tried to make this book, that will always be at the back of my mind: but, were they alive today, they would have been first to join in the laughter, and that laughter was, I'm sure, the key to victory.

Prologue

After *Puckoon* I swore I would never
write another novel. This is it . . .

Part one

HOW IT ALL STARTED

September 3rd, 1939. The last minutes of peace ticking away. Father and I were watching Mother digging our air-raid shelter. "She's a great little woman," said Father. "And getting smaller all the time," I added. Two minutes later, a man called Chamberlain who did Prime Minister impressions spoke on the wireless; he said, "As from eleven o'clock we are at war with Germany." (I loved the *WE*.) "War?" said Mother. "It must have been something we said," said Father. The people next door panicked, burnt their post office books and took in the washing.

The air-raid shelter my mother built for the family. The face is my father's

Giant troop-carrying submarines

Almost immediately came the mournful wail of the first Air-Raid Warning. "Is that you dear?" said Mother. "It's a Jewish Funeral," said Father, "Quick! Put out the begging bowls." It was in fact the Bata Shoe Factory lunch hooter. It caused chaos until it was changed. Uncle Willie, a pre-death mortician, who hadn't worked for years, started making small wooden mushrooms. He sent them to Air-Marshal Harris requesting

Giant troop-carrying airships

266-ton land cruiser (upper and lower decks)

they be dropped on Germany to prove that despite five days of war, British craftsmanship still flourished. They were returned with a note saying, "Dropping wooden mushrooms during raids might cause unnecessary injury." My brother Desmond too, seized with pre-pubic patriotism, drew pictures of fantastic war machines. He showed Father: "Son," he said, "these inventions will be the salvation of England." They wasted no time: carrying the portfolio of drawings in a string bag, they hurried to Whitehall by 74 tram. After several arguments and a scuffle, they were shown into the presence of a curious nose-

Schoolboy's impression of how Britain should meet the invader: tanks meeting high tension wires (looking like barbed wire) and exploding on contact

manipulating Colonel. He watched puzzled as Father laid out drawings of Troop-Carrying Submarines, Tank-Carrying Zeppelins and some of Troops on Rocket-Propelled Skates, all drawn on the backs of old dinner menus. "Right," said the Colonel, "I'll have the brown windsor, roast beef and two veg." Father and son were then shown the door, the windows, and finally the street. My father objected. "You fool! By rejecting these inventions you've put two years on the war." "Good," said the Colonel, "I wasn't doing anything!" Father left. With head held high and feet held higher, he was thrown out.

He took the war very seriously; as time went on so did Neville Chamberlain, he took it so seriously he resigned. "Good! He's stepping down for a better man," concluded Father, and wrote off for the job. One Saturday morning, while Mother was at church doing a bulk confession for the family, Father donned an old army uniform and proceeded to transform the parlour into H.Q. Combined Ops. Walls were covered in tatty maps. On the table was a 1927 map of Thomas Tilling's bus routes. Using wooden mushrooms as anti-tank guns, Uncle Willie placed them at various points on the map for the defence of Brockley. My father told the early morning milkman, "That," he said tapping the map, "that is where they'll start their attack on England."

"That's Africa," said the puzzled Milkman.

"Ah yes!" said Father, quick to recover, "But that's where they'll start from – Africa – understand?"

"No I don't," said the Milkman. Where upon he was immediately nipped in the scrotum, thrown out, and his horse whipped into a gallop. "Only two pints tomorrow," Father shouted after the disappearing cart.

Next morning a Constable arrived at the door.

"Ah, good morning Constable," said Father raising his steel helmet. "You're just in time."

"In time for what sir?"

"In time for me to open the door for you," said Father, reeling helplessly with laughter.

"Very funny sir," said the Constable.

"Knew you'd like it," said Father, wiping tears from his eyes.

"Now what can we do for you, a robbery? a murder? I mean times must be bad for the force, why not slap a writ on Hitler?"

"It's about these barricades you put across the road."

"Oh? What's wrong with them? We're at war you know."

"It's not me sir, it's the tram drivers. They're shagged out having to lift them to get through, they've got to come down."

"You're all fools!" said Father, "I'll write to Churchill." He did. Churchill told him to take them down as well.

"He's a bloody fool too," said Father. "If he's not careful I'll change sides."

My father, Leo Milligan   *Grandfather William Milligan*

I was no stranger to Military Life. Born in India on the Regimental strength, the family on both sides had been Gunners as far back as the Seige of Lucknow. Great-Grandfather, Sergeant John Henry Kettleband, had been killed in the Indian Mutiny, by his wife, his last words were, "Oh!" His father had died in a military hospital after being operated on for appendi-

Great-grandfather Michael Milligan

My mother's side. Trumpet Sergeant A. H. Kettleband, Indian Army, about 1899

citis by a drunken doctor. On the tombstone was carved –

R.I.P.

In memory of
Sgt. Thomas Kettleband.
954024731.

Died of appendicitis
for his King & Country.

Now apparently it was my turn.

One day an envelope marked O.H.M.S. fell on the mat. Time for my appendicitis, I thought.

"For Christ's sake don't open it," said Uncle, prodding it with a stick. "Last time I did, I ended up in Mesopotamia, chased by Turks waving pots of Vaseline and shouting, 'Lawrence we love you in Ottoman'."

Father looked at his watch, "Time for another advance," he said and took one pace forward. Weeks went by, several more O.H.M.S. letters arrived, finally arriving at the rate of two a day stamped URGENT.

"The King must think a lot of you son, writing all these letters," said Mother as she humped sacks of coal into the cellar. One Sunday, while Mother was repointing the house, as a treat Father opened one of the envelopes. In it was a cunningly worded invitation to partake in World War II, starting at seven and sixpence a week, all found. "Just fancy," said Mother as she carried Father upstairs for his bath, "of all the people in England, they've chosen you, it's a great honour, son."

Laughingly I felled her with a right cross.

I managed to delay the fatal day. I'll explain. Prior to the war, I was a keep-fit addict. Every morning you could see people counting the bones in my skinny body at Ladywell Recreation Track, as I lifted barbells. Sometimes we were watched by admiring girls from Catford Labour Exchange; among them was one with a tremendous bosom. She looked like the Himalayas on their side. The sight of this released some kind of sex hormones into my being that made me try to lift some impossible weight to impress her. Loading the barbell to one hundred and sixty pounds (about $70) I heaved at the weights, Kerrrrrrissttt!! an agonised pain shot round my back into my groin, down my leg, and across the road to a bus stop. Crippled and trying to grin, I crawled, cross-eyed with agony, towards the shower rooms. Screams of laughter came from the girls.

"Ohhh yes," said our neighbour Mrs Windust, "you've got a rupture comin'. My 'usband 'ad one from birth. Orl fru our courtin' days 'e managed to keep it a secret, 'course, on our 'oneymoon 'e 'ad to show me, and then I saw 'e was 'eld together wiv a Gathorne and Olins advanced leather truss. 'e 'ad to 'ave

21

Tommy Brettell's Ritz Revels. Yours truly, extreme right,
front row

it remodelled before we could 'ave sectional intercourse."

Terrified, I hied me to my Hearts of Oak Sick Benefit Hindu
Doctor, who had a practice in Brockley Rise. "Oh yes Milligan!
You are getting a rupture! I can feel it!" he said inserting curry-
stained fingers like red hot pokers in my groin. That diagnosis
from a son of the B.M.A. was thirty-five years ago. I'm not
ruptured yet. Perhaps I'm a late starter. Rupture! the thought
filled me with lumps of fear, why? For three years I had been
trumpet player with the Ritz Revels, a bunch of spotty musicians
held together with hair oil. They paid ten shillings a gig;*
of this I gave Mother nine, who in turn gave seven to the church
for the Poor of the Parish. I couldn't understand it, *we* were the
Poor of the Parish.

Blowing a trumpet puts a strain on the groin up to chest
height, so, everytime we did a gig I improvised a truss. I stuffed
rags into an old sock until it was packed tight. I then placed it
in the predicted rupture spot and attached it to my groin with
lengths of tape and string, this gave me a bulge in my trousers
that looked like the erection of a stallion. Something had to be

* A one night stand

done, I mean, if some woman saw it, I could never live up to it, so I tried to reduce the bulge by putting leather straps round me and pulling them tight; nothing happened except my voice went up an octave. It still looked obscene, but Mother came to the rescue; she sewed on an additional length of dyed black curtain which covered the bulge but brought the jacket half way down my thighs. Embarrassed, I explained it away by saying, "This is the latest style from America, Cab Calloway wears one." "He must be a cunt," said the drummer.

I had bought the evening dress from my Uncle Alf of Catford for thirty-eight shillings, the suit was tight, but so was money, so I bought it. For weeks I played in my leather harness trussed up like a Turkey.

After a month I got saddle sores and went to the doctor, who passed me on to a vet, in turn, he reported me to the police as a Leather Pervert. The pain in my back persisted, sometimes I couldn't move for it. What I had was a slipped disc, a condition then unknown to the world of medicine. But to get a 'bad back' at the same time as your call-up rings as hollow as a naked wife in bed with the lodger saying the laundry's late. (In my case it was true, the laundry was late.) I was put in Lewisham General Hospital under observation. I think a nurse did it through a hole in the ceiling. Specialists seeking security in numbers came in bunches of four to examine me. They prodded me, then stepped back to see what happened. "He's still alive," said one. They then hit me all over with rubber mallets and kept saying to each other "what do you think?" Days later a card arrived saying "Renal Colic".

The old man in the next bed leaned over and said in a hoarse voice, "Git aht of here son. I come in 'ere wiv vericose veins and they took me 'pendix aht."

"Thanks," I said, "my name's Milligan."

"Mine's Ethel Martin," he said.

"Ethel? It says Dick on your chart."

"I was when I come in, somewhere between there and 'ere."
He pointed in an obvious direction.

"The unkindest cut of all?"

"They got me mixed up with someone who wanted to be

1982°

19 mar. 40

London County Council—Public Health Department.

LEWISHAM HOSPITAL.

For use of Almoner	HSM.
Case No. **4437**	

OUT-PATIENT ATTENDANCE CARD

of (name) _Terence Milligan_

Seen by Almoner	
Dates	Initials
19.3.40	h

(address) _50 Riseldine_

_Rd. S.E._

(date) _9 . 3 . 40_

(Initials) ....

Sister.

5000 (F11184-376) 19.6.39

Seen by Almoner		Times for out-patient attendances
Dates	Initials	D? Muscle Strain (See ward
		? Renal Colic) Notes
		Discharged from D.I. 9/3/4
		To Mr. Darling's O.P.D.
		12/3/40 . 2 pm.

3 Jan 1940

NATIONAL SERVICE (ARMED FORCES) ACT, 1939

GRADE CARD

Registration No. *LNK/344*

Mr. *Milligan, Terence Alan*

whose address on his registration card is

50, Riseldine Rd. SE23

was medically examined at **RECRUITING CENTRE 16 ELTHAM.**

on **31 JAN '40**

> **LEWISHAM**
> **MEDICAL BOARD (No. 1)**

and placed in

GRADE* *I (one)*

E.D. Until

(Medical Board stamp.)

Chairman of Board *E. J. B. Buchan.*

Man's Signature *Ted Milligan*

---

*The roman numeral denoting the man's Grade (with number also spelt out) will be entered in RED ink by the Chairman himself, e.g., Grade I (one), Grade II (two) (a) (Vision). If the examination is deferred the Chairman will enter a date after the words " E.D. Until ", and cross out " Grade " ; alternatively, the words " E.D. Until............ " will be struck out.

N.S. 55   [P.T.O.

sterilized. How do you tell your wife you ain't what she thinks you are?"

"Don't tell her, show her!"

"I'll think about it."

"From now on that's all you will be able to do about it."

Those sons of fun at the hospital, having failed to diagnose my ailment, discharged me with a letter recommending electrical treatment, and headed "To whom it may concern" – I suppose that meant me. It was now three months since my call-up. To celebrate I hid under the bed dressed as Florence Nightingale. Next morning I received a card asking me to attend a medical at the Yorkshire Grey, Eltham. "Son," said Father, "I think after all you better go, we're running out of disguises, in any case when they see you, they're bound to send you home." The card said I was to report at 9.30 a.m. "Please be prompt." I arrived prompt at 9.30 and was seen promptly at 12.15. We were told to strip. This revealed a mass of pale youths with thin, white, hairy legs. A press photographer was stopped by the recruiting Sergeant. "For Christ's sake don't! If the public saw a photo of this lot they'd pack it in straight away." I arrived in the presence of a grey-faced, bald doctor.

"How do you feel?" he said.

"All right," I said.

"Do you feel fit?"

"No, I walked here."

Grinning evilly, he wrote Grade 1 (One) in blood red ink on my card. "No black cap?" I said. "It's at the laundry," he replied.

The die was cast. It was a proud day for the Milligan family as I was taken from the house. "I'm too young to go," I screamed as Military Policemen dragged me from my pram, clutching a dummy. At Victoria Station the R.T.O. gave me a travel warrant, a white feather and a picture of Hitler marked "This is your enemy." I searched every compartment, but he wasn't on the train. At 4.30, June 2nd, 1940, on a summer's day all mare's tails and blue sky we arrived at Bexhill-on-Sea, where I got off. It wasn't easy. The train didn't stop there.

Part two

I JOIN THE REGIMENT

Lugging a suitcase tied with traditional knotted string, I made my way to Headquarters 56th Heavy Regiment Royal Artillery. Using sign language they re-directed me to D Battery. They were stationed in a building called "Worthingholm", an evacuated girls' school in Hastings Road. As I entered the drive, a thing of singular military ugliness took my eye. It was Battery Sergeant-Major 'Jumbo' Day. His hair was so shorn his neck seemed to go straight up the back of his hat, and his face was suffused red by years of drinking his way to promotion. "Oi! Where yew goin'? It ain't a girls' school no more."
"Isn't it? Never mind I'll join the Regiment instead," I said.
He screwed up his eyes. "You're not *Milligan*, are yew?"
"Actually I am."
A beam of sadistic pleasure spread over his face.
"We've been waiting for yew!" he said, pushing me ahead of him with his stick. He drove me into what was D Battery Office. The walls once white were now thrice grey. From a peeling ceiling hung a forty watt bulb that when lit made the room darker. A Janker Wallah was giving the bare floor a stew-coloured hue by slopping a mop around, re-arranging the dirt. On the wall was a calendar with a naked tart advertising cigarettes. Below it was a newspaper cut-out of Neville Chamberlain grinning upwards. Fronting the fireplace was a trestle table covered with a merry grey blanket. A pile of O.H.M.S. letters, all addressed to me, were tucked in the corner of the blotter. In the lid of a cardboard shoe-box was a collection of rubber bands, paper-clips, sealing-wax, string and a lead weight. My pulses raced! Here was the heart of a great fighting machine. Seated behind this mighty war organ was a middle-aged, pink, puffy-faced man in his early fifties wearing a uniform in its late seventies. Parts that had frayed had been trimmed with leather; these included cuffs, elbows, pockets, gaiters and all trailing edges; for this reason he was known as 'Leather Suitcase'. His maiden name was Major Startling-Grope. "This is Gunner Milligan sir," said the B.S.M. When they'd both finished laughing, the Major spoke.

29

*Very well, alone then! Gnr. Milligan, 954024, defending
England, June 1940*

"Whair hev yew been, and whai are yew wearing civilian clothes?"

"They wouldn't let me on the train naked sir."

"I mean, whai aren't you in uniform?"

"I'm not at war with anybody sir."

"Silence when you speak to an officer," said B.S.M.

The Major, who was fiddling with a rubber band, slid it over his finger.

"Does this mean we're engaged sir?"

"Silence!" said B.S.M.

"I suppose," said Suitcase, "you know you are three months late arriving?"

"I'll make up for it sir, I'll fight nights as well!" All these attempts at friendly humour fell on stony ground. I was marched to a bare room by a Bombardier. He pointed to a floor board.

"You're trying to tell me something," I said.

"Your bed, right?"

"Right."

"Right *Bombardier*!"

"I'm a Bombardier already?"

"Oh cheeky bastard, eh? Got the very job for yew."

He gave me a scrubbing-brush with two bristles, showed me a three acre cook-house floor and pointed down; he was still trying to tell me something. Leering over all this was the dwarf-like Battery Cook, Bombardier Nash, who looked like Quasimodo with the hump reversed. He was doing things to sausages. Three hours' scrubbing, and the knees in my trousers went through. To make matters worse there were no uniforms in the 'Q' stores. I cut a racy figure on guard, dark blue trousers gone at the knee, powder blue double-breasted chalk-stripe jacket, lemon shirt and white tie, all set off with steel helmet, boots and gaiters. It wasn't easy.

"Halt! Who goes there?" I'd challenge. When they saw me the answer was, "Piss Off." I had to be taken off guard duties. In time I got a uniform. It made no difference.

"Halt, who goes there?"

"Piss Off."

Words can't describe the wretched appearance of a soldier

in a new battle-dress. Size had nothing to do with it. You wore
what you got. Some soldiers never left barracks for fear of
being seen. Others spent most of their time hiding behind trees.
The garments were impregnated with an anti-gas agent that
reeked like dead camels, and a water-proofing chemical that
gave you false pregnancy and nausea. The smell of 500 newly
kitted rookies could only be likened to an open Hindu sewer-
age works on a hot summer night by Delius. To try and 'cure'
my B.D. I salted it and hung it outside in thunderstorms, I took
it for walks, I hit it, in desperation, I sprayed it with Eau de
Cologne, it made little difference, except once a sailor followed
me home. Overcoats were a huge, shapeless dead loss. If you
wanted alterations, you took it to a garage. But the most difficult part of Army Life was the 06:00 hours awakening. In films
this was done by a smart bugler who, silhouetted against the
dawn with the Union Jack flying, blew reveille. Not so our
'Badgey',* who stayed in bed, pushed the door open with his
foot, blew reveille, then went back to sleep.

DUNKIRK

The first eventful date in my army career was the eve of the
final evacuation from Dunkirk, when I was sent to the O.P. at
Galley Hill to help the cook. I had only been in the Army
twenty-four hours when it happened. Each news bulletin from
BBC told an increasingly depressing story. Things were
indeed very grave. For days previously we could hear the
distant sound of explosions and heavy gunfire from across the
Channel. Sitting in a crude wood O.P. heaped with earth at
two in the morning with a Ross Rifle with only five rounds
made you feel so bloody useless in relation to what was going
on the other side. Five rounds of ammo, and that was between
the *whole* O.P. The day of the actual Dunkirk evacuation the
Channel was like a piece of polished steel. I'd never seen a sea

* Badgey: Bugler

32

Dotted line shows actual size of body

← ALWAYS TOO BIG. ALSO LETS IN RAIN, SNOW WIND, SOUP.

LONG SLEEVES GET IN SOUP.

SOUP AND WIND GETS UP HERE.

SOUP CATCHES HERE ←

Standard English battle-dress

The O.P., Galley Hill, with the coast-guard and fishermen's cottages at the back

so calm. One would say it was miraculous. I presume that something like this had happened to create the "Angel of Mons" legend. That afternoon Bombardier Andrews and I went down for a swim. It would appear we were the only two people on the south coast having one. With the distant booms, the still sea, and just two figures on the landscape, it all seemed very very strange. We swam in silence. Occasionally, a squadron of Spitfires or Hurricanes headed out towards France. I remember so clearly, Bombardier Andrews standing up in the water, putting his hands on his hips, and gazing towards where the B.E.F. was fighting for its life. It was the first time I'd seen genuine concern on a British soldier's face; "I can't see how they're

34

going to get 'em out," he said. We sat in the warm water for a while. We felt so helpless. Next day the news of the "small armada" came through on the afternoon news. As the immensity of the defeat became apparent, somehow the evacuation turned it into a strange victory. I don't think the nation ever reached such a feeling of solidarity as in that week at any other time during the war. Three weeks afterwards, a Bombardier Kean, who had survived the evacuation, was posted to us. "What was it like," I asked him.

"Like son? It was a fuck up, a highly successful fuck up."

SUMMER 1940

> Apples be ripe
> Nuts be brown
> Petticoats up
> Trousers down (*Old Sussex Folk Song*)

Apart from light military training in Bexhill there didn't seem to be a war on at all, it was a wonderful 'shirts off' summer. Around us swept the countryside of Sussex. There were the August cornfields that gave off a golden halitus, each trembling ear straining up for the sun. The Land Girls looked brown and inviting and promised an even better harvest. On moonlight nights haystacks bore lovers through their primitive course, by day there was shade a-plenty, oaks, horse chestnuts, willows, all hung out hot wooden arms decked with the green flags of summer.

The W.V.S. Forces Corner on the corner of Sea and Cantalupe Road, was open for tea, buns, billiards, ping-pong and deserters. The Womens' Voluntary Service girls were 'jolly nice', that is, they were undatable. We tried to bait them with Woodbines disguised in a Players packet and trying to walk like John Wayne. The other excitement was watching German planes trying to knock off the radar installations at Pevensey. Bombardier Rossi used to run a book on it. It was ten to one on against the towers being toppled. Weekends saw most officers off home in mufti. Apparently the same went for the Germans. The phoney war was on. I was now a trainee Signaller, highly inefficient in morse, flags and helio lamps. My duties were simple, a week in every month at an Observation Post over-looking the Channel. We had three: Galley Hill, Bexhill; a Martello Tower, Pevensey; and Constables Farm on the Bexhill–Eastbourne Road. Most of us tried for the Martello on Pevensey Beach as the local birds were easier to lay, but you had to be quick because of the tides. My first confrontation with the enemy was an early autumn evening at Galley Hill O.P. The light was going and a mist was conjuring itself up from the Channel. I'd just finished duty and was strolling along the cliff, enjoying a cigarette; in the absence of a piano I was whistling that bloody awful Warsaw Concerto when suddenly! Nothing happened! But it had happened suddenly, mark you. A moment later I heard the unmistakable sound of a Dornier Bomber, 103 feet long, wing span 80 feet, speed 108 m.p.h., piloted by Fritz Gruber aged twenty-three with a gold filling in his right lower molar. Suddenly, below me, coming out of the mist was the Dornier, flying low to avoid radar and customs duty. I could actually see the pilot and co-pilot's faces lit by a blue light on the instrument panel. What should I do? A pile of bricks! I grabbed one and as the plane roared over me, I threw it. Blast! Missed! But in that moment I envisaged glorious headlines. LONE GUNNER BRINGS DOWN NAZI PLANE WITH LONE BRICK . . . INVESTITURE AT PALACE. MILLIGAN M.M. And the Germans! "Mein Gott, if dis iss vot dey can do vid bricks, vot vill dey get vid guns?" They didn't all get away. That week a Hurricane downed a Dornier on Peven-sey marsh. We ran to the crash. It was going to be a bad year for the rear gunner, he was dead. The young blond pilot was being treated by the Battery Cook, Gunner Sherry, who had been discharged from the Army on grounds of Insanity, then invited to join up again on the same grounds. He held the pilot with a carving-knife. We were very short of meat. Before the RAF recovery unit arrived we knocked off anything moveable, including the dead German's boots. The rear gunner's Spandau was handed to Leather Suitcase who tried to raffle it: however,

*Gunner Milligan
at the mighty
Spandau*

after discussions he decided to use it as an A.A. gun. He really
was getting the hang of things. A pit was dug outside 'Trevissick' (the officers' billets). One morning, on the last stag (04:00
to 06:00) I heard a Dornier circling in low cloud. What a chance!
I uncovered the Spandau. I could see the headlines again,
MILLIGAN DOWNS ANOTHER! KING TAKES BACK M.M.
IN PART EXCHANGE FOR V.C. A window opened. The
lathered face of Leather Suitcase appeared.

"Milligan? What are you standing there for?"

"Everybody's got to be somewhere sir."

"What are you doing?"

"Going to have a crack at the Hun sir."

"Don't be a bloody fool, you'll give our position away. Now
cover up that gun before it gets spoilt." As he spoke there was
a lone explosion. The Dornier had dropped a bomb in Devonshire Square.

"You see what you've done," he said, slamming the window.

He must have been worth two divisions to the Germans. It was going to be a long war. Churchill had a tough job on. It was thanks to him that we had any guns at all.

When the '14–'18 War ended, Churchill said the 9.2s were to be dismantled, put in grease and stored in case of 'future eventualities'. There was one drawback. No Ammunition. This didn't deter Leather Suitcase, he soon had all the gun crews shouting 'BANG' in unison. "Helps keep morale up," he told visiting Alanbrooke. By luck a 9.2 shell was discovered in Woolwich Rotunda. An official application was made: in due course the shell arrived. A guard was mounted over it. The Mayor was invited to inspect it, the Mayoress was photographed alongside with a V for Victory sign; I don't think she had the vaguest idea what it meant. A month later, application was made to H.Q. Southern Command to fire the shell. The date was set for July 2nd, 1940. The day prior, we went round Bexhill carrying placards.

Our very own 9·2 gun howitzer   *(The Imperial War Museum)*

> # THE NOISE YOU WILL HEAR
> # TOMORROW AT MIDDAY WILL BE
> # THAT OF BEXHILL'S OWN CANNON.
> # DO NOT BE AFRAID.

Other men went round telling people to open their windows, otherwise the shock waves might break them. Even better, they were told, "Break the windows yourself and save the hanging-about." Dawn! the great day! We were marched to a secret destination on the coast known only to us, and the enemy. Freezing, with a gathering fog, we all sat in the corner of a windy beach that was forever England. They told us, "Listen for the bang and look for the splash." Before the visiting brass arrived the fog had obscured the view. The order now became *Listen* for the splash. Zero hour. Tension mounting. A Lance Bombardier was arrested for sneezing. A Jewish gunner fainted on religious grounds. Lieutenant Budden was stung by a bee; lashing out with his hand, he struck Captain Martin's pipe, driving the stem down his throat, leaving just the bowl protruding from his lips and fumigating his nose. Disaster! Sergeant Dawson, A.I.* of Signals, reported the line to the gun position had got a break. Signallers Devine and White, who would do anything for a break, set off. In the haste to defend the Sceptered Isle, the South Coast was a mass of hurriedly-laid, unlabelled telephone lines, along walls, down drains, up men's trouser legs, everywhere!

After thirty military minutes, the O.P. telephone buzzed.

"Ah!" said Dawson hopefully, "O.P. here."

"We haven't found the break yet."

"Right. Keep trying."

The fog was now settling inland. Top brass had finished the contents of their thermos flasks and withdrawn to the shelter of a deserted fisherman's cottage. All was silent save the sound of frozen gunners singing the International. Every ten minutes for two hours, Signaller Devine phoned and gleefully reported, "line still broken, Sarge." The fog was very dense, as were Signallers Devine and White, who were now groping their way through Sussex in Braille. C.O.'s patience being exhausted, a runner was sent to the gun position. Off went Gunner Balfour, the Battery champion athletes foot. Another hour. He was lost. In despair Sergeant Dawson bicycled to the police station, telephoned the Gun Position and told them "Fire the Bloody Thing!" A distant 'BOOM'. At the O.P. we heard the whistle as the rare projectile passed overhead into the Channel, a pause, a splash, then silence . . . it was a dud. How could the Third Reich stand up to this punishment! Next day at low tide we were sent out to look for traces of the lost projectile; we didn't, but it was a nice day for that sort of thing.

* Assistant Instructor

Left to right: Gunners Edgington, Milligan, White and Devine, at low tide on the beach at Galley Hill O.P., Bexhill, the day after the famous dud shell was fired, looking for traces of the lost projectile

LIFE IN BEXHILL 1940–41

In Bexhill life carried on. We went on route marches which became pleasant country walks. A favourite marching song was 'Come inside' – so:

Verse: Outside a lunatic asylum one day
        A Gunner was picking up stones;
        Up popped a lunatic and said to him,
        Good Morning Gunner Jones,
        How much a week do you get for doing that?
        Fifteen bob, I cried.
        He looked at me
        With a look of glee
        And this is what he cried,

Chorus: Come inside, you silly bugger, come inside,
       I thought you had a bit more sense,
       Working for the Army, take my tip
       Act a bit balmy and become a lunatic;
       You get your four meals regular
       and two new suits beside,
       Wot? fifteen bob a week,
       A wife and kids to keep,
       Come inside, you silly bugger, come inside.

No matter what season, the Sussex countryside was always a pleasure. But the summer of 1941 was a delight. The late lambs on springheel legs danced their happiness. Hot, immobile cows chewed sweet cud under the leaf-choked limbs of June oaks that were young 500 years past. The musk of bramble and blackberry hedges, with purple-black fruit offering themselves to passing hands, poppies red, red, red, tracking the sun with open-throated petals, birds bickering aloft, bibulous to the sun. White fleecy clouds passing high, changing shapes as if uncertain of what they were. To break for a smoke, to lie in that beckoning grass and watch cabbage white butterflies dancing on the wind. Everywhere was saying bethankit. It was hop picking time. In 1941 the pickers were real cockneys who, to the consternation of the A.R.P. Wardens, lit bonfires at night and sang roistering songs under the stars. "Right, fags out, fall in!" – of course, I almost forgot, the war! but people were saying it would all be over by Christmas. Good! that was in twelve weeks' time! I started to read the 'Situations Vacant' in the *Daily Telegraph*, and prematurely advertised, 'Gunner 954024, retired house-trained war hero, unexpectedly vacant. Can pull a piece of string and shout bang with confidence.'

Part three

I took my trumpet to war. I thought I'd earn spare cash by playing Fall In, Charge, Retreat, Lights Out, etc. I put a printed card on the Battery Notice Board, showing my scale of charges:

> Fall In 1/6
> Fall out 1/–
> Charge. 1/9
> Halt £648
> Retreat (Pianissimo). 4/–
> Retreat (Fortissimo) 10/–
> Lights Out. 3/–
> Lights Out played in private . . 4/–

While waiting for these commissions I'd lie on my palliasse and play tunes like, 'Body and Soul', 'Can't Get Started', 'Stardust'. It was with mixed feeling that I played something as exotic as 'You go to my Head' watching some hairy gunner cutting his toe-nails. Of course I soon contacted the Jazz addicts. I was introduced to six-foot-two dreamy-eyed Gunner Harry Edgington. A Londoner, he was an extraordinary man,

*Harry Edgington in
a brown study*

with moral scruples that would have pleased Jesus. It was the start of a lifelong friendship. Harry played the piano. Self taught. He delighted me with some tunes he had composed. He couldn't read music, and favoured two keys, F sharp and C sharp! both keys the terror of the Jazz man: however, over the months I'd busk tunes with him in the N.A.A.F.I. I taught him the names of various chords and he was soon playing in keys that made life easier for me. He was game for a 'Jam' any time. And of course, start to hum any tune and Harry would be in with the harmony, and spot on. It helped life a lot to have him around. One day, with nothing but money in mind, I suggested to Harry we try and form a band. Harry grinned and looked disbelieving. "Just the two of us?"

"We could sit far apart," I said.

A stroke of luck. A driver, Alf Fildes, was posted to us with suspected rabies and he played the guitar! All we needed was a drummer. We advertised in Part Two Orders. 'Wanted. House Trained Drummer. Academic Training advantage, but not essential. Apply The Gunners Milligan and Edgington. No coloureds but men with names like Duke Ellington given preference.' No one came forward. We were stuck, worse still we were stuck in the Army. But! Milligan had the eye of an eagle, the ear of a dog, and the brain of a newt, (we've all got to eat). One meal time, as the dining hall rang to the grinding of teeth on gritty cabbages, came the sound of a rhythmic beat; it was a humble gunner hammering on a piece of Lease Lend bacon, trying to straighten it out for the kill. This was Driver Douglas Kidgell. Would he like to be our drummer? Yes. Good. Now, where to get the drums. Gunner Nick Carter said there was a 'certain' drum kit lying fallow under the stage of Old Town Church Hall. Captain Martin, a sort of commissioned Ned Kelly, suggested we 'requisition' the 'certain' drum kit to prevent it falling into German hands. This sort of patriotism goes deep. With Germany poised to strike we couldn't waste time. We took the drums, and camouflaged them by painting on the Artillery Crest. Kidgell soon got the hang of the drums, and lo! we were a quartet!

After a month's practice, Captain Martin asked could we

Driver Doug Kidgell, as the Khaki Pimpernell

Driver Kidgell playing the drums as though they weren't stolen

play for a dance. I told him we had a very limited repertoire, he said "So have I, we'll hold the dance this Saturday." GAD! this was the big time! Saturday, The Old Town Church Hall, Bexhill! who knows next week, Broadway! In entertainment starved Bexhill, the dance was a sell-out. The old corrugated iron Hall was packed to suffocation; there were old women, kids, officers, gunners, various wives, very much a village dance affair.

The memorable first wartime dance in Bexhill
Old Town Church Hall, and the band's first
engagement

After twenty minutes we had exhausted our repertoire, so we started again. I suppose playing 'Honeysuckle Rose' forty times must be some kind of a record. The bar did roaring business, the barman being none other than the Reverend Clegg, Regimental Vicar. We played well on into the night. About two o'clock Captain Martin called a halt. They all stood to attention, we played 'God Save the King'. Now for the rewards. To pay us, Captain Martin led us into the Churchyard in pitch darkness. There he gave us a ten shilling note.

"A little something for you lads," he said.

"Ten bob?" said Fildes painfully. "Couldn't we raffle it?"

48

"Now then lads, remember there's a war on," said Martin pocketing the rest.

That night, by a flickering candle, we all swore allegiance to Karl Marx. No matter what, next dance, unless we got paid more, we'd play the bloody awful Warsaw Concerto!

On pay nights most of us headed for the pubs – where, apart from drinking, a lot of singing was done by the battery duet-tists, Gunners White and Devine. This was a very popular one:

> I paid my entrance fee
> To see that tattooed she
> She had Sir Hubert Tree
> Tattooed upon her knee
> She had a great big Union Jack
> Tattooed upon her back
> And down below
> On her big toe
> Jack Johnson done in black
> She had a battleship
> Tattooed upon her hip
> And where I could not see
> A map of Germany
> She had a picture of Harry Lauder
> Right across where she gets broader
> And as a mixture
> She had a picture
> Of her home in Tenersee.

White and Devine were great fans of the band and travelled everywhere with us. Devine, who fancied himself as a 'Bing Crosby' in uniform, often took vocals.

In the months to come we enlivened many a lonely military camp. We saw life. In Upper Dicker, we played for a dance-cum-orgy. Couples were disappearing into the tall grass having it off and then coming back to the dance. God knows how many Coitus Interupti the Hesitation Waltz caused, but we heard screams from behind the trees.

49

Music has strange effects on drunks: one lunatic ripped open his battle-dress, pointed to a scar on his chest, and shouted "Dunkirk! you bloody coward." He had a face made from red plasticine by a child of three, that or his parachute didn't open. "Do you hear me, you bloody coward. Dunkirk . . ." he kept saying. I've no idea what he meant. I confused him by giving him the ladies' spot prize. A fight broke out with the Canadians. They were all massive.

"How do you get such huge men?" I asked one.

"We go in the forest, shake the trees and they fall out," he said.

A worried officer rushed up.

"Can you play 'The Maple Leaf Forever'?"

"No sir, after an hour I get tired."

"You're under arrest," he said.

In despair we played The King, shouted 'Everyone back to their own beds', and departed.

On Bexhill's sea front stood the De La Warr Pavillion, named after Lord De La Warr Pavillion, a fine modern building with absolutely no architectural merit at all. It was opened just in time to be bombed. The plane that dropped it was said to have been chartered by the Royal Institute of Architects, piloted by Sir Hugh Casson with John Betjeman as bomb aimer. The invasion of England, though always imminent, did not stop the reopening of the Pavillion for dances by the local Rotary Club. The band could now play on a genuine stage, and 'N.A.A.F.I. Piano-ridden' Edgington could perform on a concert Steinway Grand. Our M.C. was Mr Courtney who was 'well known in Bexhill'. He owned an antique shop, and when short of stock put his suits in the window. Occasionally he sang 'Might Lak a Rose' in a quavering light baritone (or mighty like a baritone, in a quivering rose), which suggested a maladjusted truss. He told us he thought Charlie Kunz was the greatest Jazz pianist in the world, in his own words, "He's a sort of white Duke Ellington."

During the months leading into the winter of 1940 the D Battery were the centre of night life in war-ridden, sinful Bexhill-on-Sea. I didn't know it at the time, but I was taking the first steps into Show Business.

RELIGION

Men in uniform can't really be considered religious, unless it
be a Christian profundity that makes a Gunner say Jesus
Christ! when he drops a shell on his foot. Even the Battery
Chaplain was suspect. One night I found him face downwards
near the Officers Billets, singing 'The Lord is my Shepherd';
granted, it may have been a new way of holding services during
heavy shelling. The Catholics had occasional visits from
Father Holything who seemed horrified at the thought of any
soldier having sexual intercourse.

"Be careful of strong drink my sons," he warned. "Bear in
mind it excites the sexual appetites, therefore if you see a
comrade drunk, bring him home and bathe the parts in cold
water." It was great to know how to be a Christian, all you
needed was an erection and a bucket of cold water. He warned,
"Avoid loose women." I never told him straight the women I
knew were so loose they were falling to bits. Anyway, we had
nothing to do with loose women, we were all sleeping with
highly respectable officers' wives, whose husbands were at the
war. In our rough soldier way we were trying to comfort them.
One man was comforting so many he was excused clothes.

FOOD

Oh those military meals! Breakfast could be recognised by
shape, sausage, yes, but lunch! The white watery mound could
be spuds, but what was the heap of steaming green and black,
and that knoll of boiled grey stuff that shuddered if it saw you.
Visits from orderly officers did little to help.
Officer: Any complaints?
Soldier: Yes sir, it's this.
Officer: What's wrong with 'this'.
Soldier: Nothing wrong but what is it?

Officer calls the head cook.

Officer: Sergeant. This man wants to know what this is.

Cook: That sir, is a 'Frappe Mystique à la Aldershot!'

We implemented our meals in the N.A.A.F.I. with Cornish pasties, or the eternal doughnuts. In early days doughnuts were liberally dusted with castor sugar, but as war went on that stopped. War was coming nearer even for doughnuts. The cook-house staff consisted of two ex-dustmen and the 'Chef', Sergeant Paddy Harris, with multiple B.O., black finger-nails and halitosis; medieval court poisoners couldn't have picked a more lethal trio. I could never help feeling they were paid by the Ministry of Bacteriological Warfare. Sergeant Harris was a regular. He went every morning without fail. In 1923 he was down-graded to B.2 because of varicose veins that made his legs look like maps of England's Inland Waterways. Still a citizen of the Republic, he spent his leave in Dublin. As far as the Irish were concerned, he was sabotaging the British war effort, and the way he cooked they weren't far out. Every evening, Harris could be seen leaving the billet, his Service Dress stuffed with tins of fruit, cream, and other wartime goodies that he laid at the feet of his mistress prior to coitus. When he first met her, she was a little six stone darling; when we left Bexhill two years later she weighed fourteen stone and owned a chain of grocery stores.

In 1940 he returned from leave with a piglet in his kit-bag. He intended to fatten the animal, and serve it to the Battery for Christmas dinner in exchange for some simple seasonal gift, like fifteen shillings a portion. The pig was called Brian Boru. I asked why. "Why?" said Harris sitting up in his reeking bed. "To keep alive the legend of a King." He threw up his right arm in a romantic gesture, at the same time scratching his arse with his romantic left. He stood up pulling on shattered, semen-ridden underpants: "The blood of kings runs through all Irishmen." He opened the window and spat: "You dirty bugger" came a cry from below. Harris's billet was . . . well, it appeared to have been bombed by block-busters filled with unemptied Arab dust-bins. The only thing of any merit was a picture of Jesus stuck up with a drawing pin; it bore the legend, 'I will

Sergeant Harris's method of smuggling tinned food through the British Lines at Bexhill

bless the house in which this picture is glorified'. I wonder what went wrong. The piglet. It was housed in an old Libby's Milk box lined with rubbish. The keeping of pigs in barracks was forbidden, so Harris gave the creature two coats of white paint with patches of brown that near as dammit made it look like a Cocker Spaniel. The pig got bigger and had to be re-painted as a Great Dane. At night it went foraging. Lieutenant Budden awoke one night. He phoned the guard house. "Am I drunk?" he enquired. "No sir," said the duty N.C.O. "In which case," said Budden, "there's a pig painted brown eating my boots."

We tried to tether the animal but it broke the chain. There was only one solution, dig a pit six foot deep and drop the animal in; sensing our intentions it broke free, and dashed squealing over the football pitch. Seeing our Christmas dinner disappearing, we gave chase. Heading up the road to St Leonards it suddenly turned right. "No! My God, no!" said Bombardier Donaldson as the pig rushed up the steps and through the front door of the "Belgravia Guest House for Refined Gentlefolk." Screams issued forth, crockery was breaking. Entering the hall we saw chaos! A bald man lying face down on his back with a grandfather clock across him. A fat bursting woman was clutching a gross of Pekinese; "My darlings," she trilled through a rouged hole. On the landing a fine old man with a rolled newspaper was flailing away at nothing and shouting "Shoooooo." A toothless crone issued forth stirring a sauce-pan of thrice-watered porridge. Behind her a blind man holding up sagging trousers appeared at the W.C. door. "There's no paper, Mrs Hurdle," he said. "In the cellar!" screamed a re-fined voice. Down we raced. Up we came, with the blind man bound hand and foot, still looking for paper. "It's the wrong one," said Harris. Down we raced again. A woman on the top stair kept shouting, "Mind my bottled quinces." At last we got the animal up. We were covered in cuts, bruises and bottled quince. The pig was unmarked. With a noose around his neck he was as quiet as a lamb. "Who," said a vast landlady, "who is gwoing to pway fwor all this dwamage! eh?" Sergeant Harris, braces dangling, bowed low. "That's no bloody good," she said.

"Madam, every last penny will be repaid," said Harris. He took her vile hand, kissed it, passing on his hereditary gingivitis. Somewhere on the steppes of Russia squadrons of Red tanks were advancing on all fronts. But England too was in there somewhere.

Hastings had had the pleasure of sounding their sirens about fifty times – Eastbourne about forty, but Bexhill sulked unrecognised. Then it came.

A Wednesday night, late in March 1940, the band was doing a gig at a private house in Pevensey Drive. A well heeled ex-army major was throwing a house party on the occasion of his daughter's coming-of-age. It had the cobwebs of a dying empire: men wore slightly dated evening dress, and there was one joker from the Blues with Cavalry spurs; the ladies were in gowns of chiffon that seemed straight from the wardrobe of *Private Lives*. It was pretty horsey, but not outrageously so, though I'm glad to say the moment we played a 6/8 they all did 'cocking of the legs'* and shouted 'Och Ayes'. As a parting gift our host gave us each a fiver. We stood stunned. "I'm sorry," said Kidgell, "we haven't any change sir." He waved us off. Outside, in the dark, we loaded our gear on to the fifteen hundredweight truck. Looking up I saw the night was alive with stars. In the Eastern sky I could make out Saturn, Pegasus, Castor and Pollux. I could hear the distant sound of sea washing the pebbled beaches of Pevensey. The Romans must have heard it once. We drove back in silence until Alf Fildes spoke. "Five pounds? He'll ask for it back when he sobers up!" It was gone one o'clock when we rolled ourselves in our blankets for the 'big black' (as Kidgell called sleep): we drifted off talking about the gig.

"Did you see that twit trying to do the Big Apple – what about that bird with the big Bristols! – I must of had six doubles – Five pounds! – Cor! Wish we had more gigs like that! For Christ's sake don't tell Martin, he'll confiscate it – Lovely piano – Here! you got lost in the middle eight of 'Undecided' –

* An English version of the Highland Fling, see page 102

I don't know what happened – I thought I was playing 'Hot and Anxious' . . ." gradually the talk faded – silence – night; but the time for Bexhill's siren was nigh! Somewhere in the wee wee hours a voice, "Everybody on parade at the double!" The voice of Sergeant Dawson bellowed us awake. The local air-raid sirens were going. At last! Bexhill had come into the war! In the dark we stumbled into our clothes: "Steel helmets, gas capes and respirators on!" roared a voice.

"Oh, Christ!" said Devine, "we're going to be bombed and gassed."

"Thank God!, I couldn't stand this all again."

"Come on," urged Dawson, "don't fuck about." My Mickey Mouse watch* said 3.30 a.m.! Christ!

We were trooped into the Naffi Hut, faceless in gas masks, cocooned in gas capes, the epitome of Military Efficiency. Nobody knew who was who. What must have been the B.S.M. held up the nominal roll board and was calling the names out when he realised he couldn't be heard. He raised the gas mask and started to re-call the roll: we answered but likewise, in turn, we couldn't be heard. Captain Martin, who'd had enough, took off his mask: "All take your masks off or we'll be here all bloody night."

The roll was called.

"Right! gas masks on again!"

We all stood like dummies. We could hear no planes. Several minutes passed. B.S.M. slipped his mask up: "Stand at Ease." We stood at ease. Several more minutes passed. Leather Suit-case arrived on the scene looking flushed and pissed with his pyjamas showing out of the bottoms of his trousers. For his benefit B.S.M. called the roll again. There we stood. This was our first air-raid warning. It became evident that, having roused us, nobody quite knew what to do with us. Sirens were going the length of the South Coast. "It's all Bexhill's bloody fault," said Chalky White. Eventually the eye-pieces on Suit-case's gas mask steamed up: he removed it and looked at his

*I won this by entering a colouring contest in *Mickey Mouse Weekly*! I put my age down as eleven and won a prize watch. "Well, I think that's enough" he said. "Parade dismiss Sarn't-Major," and we all trooped off to bed.

APPLICATION FOR RAF PILOT

About now, of course, the heroes of the war were the R.A.F. Pilots. It made you green with envy on leave. All the beautiful birds went out with pilots. I couldn't stand it any more. I volunteered for the Air Force. I had to be interviewed by Leather Suitcase.

"I hear you want a transfer, Milligan."

"Yes sir, I want to join the R.A.F."

"Ah yes, those are the ones that fly."

"Yes sir, they go up whereas we just go along."

"Have you ever flown before?"

"No sir, but I've been upstairs on a bus on my own."

"No, what I said was, have you ever flown before. I didn't say anything about buses."

"No sir, I have never flown before."

"Your father has written to me about it, and I will recommend you for a transfer."

In February 1941 I was called for an interview to Kingsway House. I waited in a room with about forty other hopefuls. After an hour I was called before a man who appeared to be wearing a pair of hairy outstretched wings under his nose.

"I see you want to join the R.A.F."

"Yes, sir, I have the character and temperament that is admirably suited to that arm."

"What would you like to be."

"A pilot, sir."

"Want to go out with pretty girls, eh?"

After a stringent Physical Examination they told me. "Sorry, your eyesight isn't up to what we need for a pilot; however, we have a number of vacancies for rear gunners."

"No sir, I don't want to be at the back, I want to drive."

"I'm sorry lad, that's all we can offer you."

```
                                    Trevissick,
                                    The Highlands,
                                    Bexhill.
                                    23.1.41.
Dear Sir,
          I thank you for your letter dated 20th Jan. on
the subject of your Son's transfer to the R.A.F.

          I appreciate your views and agree that with his
character and temperament he is admirably suited for ser-
vice with the air arm, and I shall be only too pleased to
assist in this transfer by giving him a strong recommenda-
tion.

          I would point out, however, that I have only just
received his application and as the matter of selection
reats entirely with the R.A.F.authorities, it is not in my
power to accelerate the transfer, other than sending his
application through the normal channels.

          A considerable number of men in the Battery have
volunteered for service with the R.A.F. and I trust your
son will be fortunate in having an interview in the near
future.

                                    Yours Faithfully,

Lieut.L.A.Milligan,R.A.O.C.
     The Tile House,
        Lower Road,
          Fetcham, Leatherhead,            Major,R.A.
```

*Letter from my major to my
father*

I stood up, saluted smartly and exited. As I walked down the
corridor to the street, I saw what was possibly the ugliest
W.A.A.F. I had ever seen. "Hello cheeky," she said as I passed
her. Perhaps they were right, perhaps I had got bad eyesight.
I caught an evening train back to Bexhill, and arrived to be
informed by Edgington that he had read in the *Melody Maker*
that Harry Parry, of the BBC Radio Rhythm Club was holding
auditions to find the best unknown jazz musicians – the winners were to make a recording for broadcasting on the BBC.
We wrote off to Harry Parry, c/o BBC, London. We received a
reply saying could we come down on the next weekend. We

approached Leather Suitcase.

"You're going to do what?"

"Do an audition for the BBC."

"You can't join them! They're civvies!"

I explained as best I could to him, bearing in mind that contemporary opinion of jazz in those days was almost the same as that of cannabis today. However, he let me go, and the following weekend, excited out of my mind, I arrived at BBC Studios, Maida Vale. Briefly, I was picked as the best trumpet player, and along with the winning alto, trombone and tenor players, we cut a disc. The pianist for this was the then almost unknown George Shearing, and for an hour, along with Harry Parry, we recorded six sides. It was an unforgettable day for me. I felt that I had been accepted as a jazz musician, and before I left, George Shearing said, "I hope we meet and play again." Man, that was praise enough.

NIGHT OF THE FIRE RAIDS

The night of September 7th, 1940, Harry and I went to the Play-house Cinema in Western Road. It was 'Black Moonlight' with Anton Walbrook, Terence de Marney and the bloody awful Warsaw Concerto. When we came out the night was filled with what sounded like relays of German bombers headed inland. There was remarkably little Ack Ack to deter them. Cloud was low and most of the Anti-aircraft batteries were further inland, grouped around strategic cities. After a quick drink in The Devonshire we ended up at the Forces Corner to finish off the evening. I started chatting up the birds, one especially, Betty Aspnel, a plain girl who made up for it with a sensational figure, man has to be satisfied with his lot, and man! this girl had the lot. I tried to create an atmosphere of Caviar and Champagne while eating beans on toast with tea. The things soldiers did to impress girls. A gunner, with a tremendous Welsh accent, tried to make a girl believe he was an American millionaire who had thrown in his lot with the British Army. It was something to hear him say "Gee whizz baby, ain't I lucky to have joined the little old British Army. Shucks, if I hadn't I'd never have met you," with a Cardiff accent. Harry wandered up to the piano and started to play a few tunes. One of the W.V.S. girls who was serving sidled up to the piano. She was the daughter of a retired Admiral in Cooden Road. She was tall and beautiful with a County School Accent. "Can you play 'Foolish Things'?" Harry complied. At first she only hummed the tune, then started to sing. Christ! She sang a quarter tone flat the whole way through. I caught Harry's eye . . . he was suffering. Always a gentleman, Harry, at the end of her effort said, "Lovely." Encouraged, she said "Do you know 'A Pair of Silver Wings'?" Harry did. At that moment he wished he had a pair. He had to sit through some seven songs, agonisingly sung, before he escaped. "She must have cloth ears," said Harry as we walked home. The bombers were still droning over. As we approached the billets we could see a glow in the northern sky. The sound of distant ack ack could be heard. "Someone's copping it," said the sentry as we walked into the drive. "Looks like it could be Redhill," said Harry. But I had my doubts. He was the only man I knew who could get lost in his own street. After the war, when I lived at Shepherds Hill, Highgate, he said he would show me a short cut to his house in St John's Way, Archway. We walked for a hour that night, during which time we never got more than three hundred yards from my house. "I can't understand it," he said. "It's the magnetic north, it must have changed during the war." Whatever that was supposed to mean I'll never know. We climbed into bed. "I've never heard so many bombers before," said Harry. We lay in bed smoking for about quarter of an hour, then Smudger Smith came in. "Cor, it looks like the sky's on fire over there." We pulled on our trousers and climbed up on the roof. The sky was on fire. Other Gunners had joined us. We watched in silence for a while. "I fink it's London," said a cockney voice. "Could be," said another. George Vincent went down for his prismatic compass. The bearing showed the fire dead on the line to London. Mick Haymer, a Londoner, tried to phone his family, but was told there was 'disruption' on the line and all calls to London were blocked. We looked at the blaze and it seemed to be getting bigger. I think we all knew it was London. My mother, father and brother were there. I'm not sure how I felt. Helpless, I suppose. Bombardier Edser switched on the BBC Midnight News, but there was no mention of any raid. Lots of the lads from London (we were a London Regiment) found it hard to sleep that night. In the dark of our bedrooms there were attempts at reassurance.

"They've all got Anderson Shelters, they're dead safe."

"Yer, dead safe."

". . . and there's all that anti-aircraft fire . . . that keeps 'em up 'igh."

". . . and there's the Underground, nuffink could break them."

The window near my bed faced north. As I lay there, I could see the glow of the fires. The bombers were still going. Some must have been on their way back as we heard cannon fire as night fighters got onto them. What a bloody mess. Men in bombers raining death on defenceless civilians. Still, soon we'd be doing it back to them, on a scale never before imagined. For the love of me I couldn't get the feeling that I was part of this. Killing of civilians was an outrage I couldn't swallow on *any* basis, on any side. In the end there were no sides. Just living and dead. Next morning we got confirmation of the raid. I managed to get through to my father at his office in Fleet Street and he told me all was well with the family. He was a fire warden on top of the Associated Press building and had seen the whole of what looked like St Paul's on fire. The papers carried stories of how many German planes were shot down, heroism of the fire brigades, wardens, Red Cross and night fighters, etc., etc. But it didn't mention the casualties that were heavy, well heavy for that time of the war; later on it appeared that London got off extremely light.

BATTERY CHARACTERS

Some people live a nothing life: the most important thing they ever do is die. Thank God for eccentrics! Take Gunner Octavian

Neat. He would suddenly appear naked in a barrack room and say, "Does anybody know a good tailor?", or "Gentlemen – I think there's a thief in the battery." He was the bane of the Regiment. When the fancy took him he would go "on the trot." "I'm off sand-ratting,"* he'd say. A month later he would give himself up, get fourteen days detention and start all over again. Leather Suitcase was baffled. Why should an Englishman in his right mind leave a perfectly good war?

"Look Neat, why do you keep going A.W.O.L.?"

"It's something to do with the shortage of money sir." Leather Suitcase as usual gave him fourteen days, and he was remanded for a psychiatrist's report.

"I don't like the uniform," Neat told the psychiatrist.

"And what's wrong with it?"

"It's dangerous. Germans shoot at it on sight."

The report said: 'There is nothing wrong with this man. He has a wholesome fear of being shot by Germans.'

"Right," said Leather Suitcase. "We'll put you where they can't get at you, fifty-six days detention!"

"Look sir," said Neat, hopefully, "supposing I say sorry?"

"Very well, say it."

"I'm sorry, sir, *very*, VERY sorry."

"Finished? Right! fifty-six days detention!" Neat stood tottering for a moment. "May I have a last request, sir?"

"Yes."

"Would you go to Beachy Head and throw your bloody self off!" This got him another fourteen days on top of the fifty-six. After this he was posted. Where to? The Tower Armoury.

Gunner Herman Frick was our hypochondriac. He wanted out. He told the M.O., "I have got hereditary flat feet." After inspecting them the M.O. gave him three aspirins. Which is the Army way of saying you're a bloody liar. "The doctor's anti-Semitic," raged Frick. "I'll prove my feet are flat." He smeared the soles of his feet with Brylcream, then stood on a piece of paper. "There," he said holding up the print, "genuine flat feet."

---

*Sand-rat: seaside whore

62

"You're too bleeding fat, mate," said Gunner Knot. It's all
that weight that makes 'em look flat."

Outraged he replied, "I'll bloody show you it's not," and then stood on his head while two of us held up a board covered in paper while he pressed his feet against it. At which moment the orderly officer entered the room. He stood silent before the strange tableau, muttered something to the duty sergeant and left. Next morning Gunner Frick was remanded for a psychiatrist's report and Part Two Orders bore this warning: "An orderly officer has reported that certain black magic rituals are being practised in barrack rooms. This contravenes King's Rules and Regulations in that within the structure of a Regiment no secret rituals or such organisations can be allowed except Housey-Housey."

To my utter amazement there was a man in the battery who had actually been with my father's Regiment in Belgaum, India, in 1923. He said he remembered my father as the Mad Quarter-bloke, which explained a lot. 'Busty' Roberts had joined the Royal Artillery in 1914 and since then had steadily risen to the rank of Gunner. Now the crunch: someone with a perverted sense of humour made him a Lance Bombardier. Roberts went insane with power. The war now consisted of two people, him and Hitler. His command of the language gave off some classic gaffs. "It's invenerial to me, sir." Books: "I like to read friction." He was the supreme bullshitter. He would sleep to attention, polish his cap badge on both sides. Cleaning his rifle one day he pulled the trigger and sent a bullet through the roof; at once he put himself on a charge. Other than a firing squad the C.O. didn't know what to do with him – finally he was posted.*

A night freak was Gunner Lichenstein: he'd suddenly sit bolt upright in bed, shout "Oh, the Goats," then lie down again. Gunner 'Spiv' Convine would dip a sleeping man's hand in a bucket of cold water and make him widdle the bed.

There was Lance Bombardier Dodds who slept in the Q. stores. He aspired to Opera. His powerful voice, not improved by singing a quarter-tone flat, especially as he started after lights out. We decided to act. One night as he lay singing "Your tiny hand is frozen," he must have heard the door open;

* The act of being sent sideways, *see* p. 66

64

"Who is it?" he said. Hurling a bucket of water, I replied, "Puccini."

This crude military life was terrible for our Jehovah's Witness, Bombardier MacDonald. Through all the vulgarity and blasphemy his voice would come out of the darkness. "I tell ye all repent! The day of judgement is at hand! Armageddon is nigh, only they that believe will be saved."

"Piss off!"

"Mock ye now, but hear me! When Jehovah cometh, you will stand to be judged!"

"Bollocks."

Despite these witty replies he maintained a non-stop attack on military morals. Like most fanatics, he didn't enjoy religion, he suffered from it. Every weekend we'd find his pamphlets on our beds. A terrible end they came to. But the pressure was too much and gradually MacDonald became less and less religious: he started drinking and swearing ("I tell you the bloody day is at hand"). The end of the holy man came one revealing night. And it came to pass that Gunner James Devine was on midnight guard when he was awakened by a rhythmic thumping from the back of the coal shed. Investigation showed Bombardier MacDonald, his trousers round his ankles, having a late-night knee-trembler with a local fat girl. The noise was her head thumping against the shed as the holy man pressed home his watch-tower. Gunner Devine watched until the climax was nigh, then shouted, "Halt! Who comes there?" The effect was electric. MacDonald ran into the night shouting 'Armageddon!'* The girl, still in a sexual coma, was given Gunner Devine's rifle to hold, while he terminated her contract. Truly they also serve who stand and wait.

B.S.M. 'Jumbo' Day thought he would test the military reflex of the Battery by sounding the six G's on the bugle. The call demanded immediate muster by all ranks, but no one in this conscripted army knew that. During the next fifteen minutes, alone in a dark field, the B.S.M. blew the six G's until he had fits, a hernia, and realised the age of the horse was over. He was

* I can only presume it meant 'Arm-a-geddon out of here'

knocked out in the early Montgomery Purge. Anyhow, we had learned our lesson: we knew now what six G's on the bugle meant. Hernia, fits, and your ticket.

Gunner Mosman. He'd get blind drunk, stagger back by 23:59 hours, feel his way into the barrack room then urinate in a corner. One day a well-spoken recruit, Gunner Donald, arrived. "Do you mind if I sleep in this corner?" Of course we didn't mind. That night, we heard the sound of Mosman streaming on the sleeping form of Gunner Donald, and strange damp screams from the victim who was a mouth breather. Gunner Donald bided his time. Next night he returned the compliment full in the sleeping Norman's face. It wasn't long before Part Two Orders read: "The practice of urinating on sleeping comrades will cease forthwith." One Bombardier, who shall remain a nameless Bastard, had it in for all of us. Revenge was very sweet. One night he came in stoned out of his mind. We waited until unconsciousness set in. Removing his trousers, we carried him and his bed to a lorry. Driven with great stealth, he was deposited in the middle of Bexhill Cemetery. Next morning, he was delivered back to us by Military Police, wrapped in a blanket and foaming at the mouth.

POSTING

Posting is an evil ritual: it was with devilish glee that one unit would pass on to another a soldier who they knew to be bloody useless. However, to keep the joke going, these failures were never discharged, just posted. There must have been, at one time, thousands of these idiots, all in a state of permanent transit, spending most of their life on lorries. Lots gave lorry numbers as a forwarding address. Hundreds spent the duration on board lorries, seven were even buried on them. There is a legend that the last of these idiots was discovered as late as 1949, living on the tail-board of a burnt-out ammunition lorry in a Wadi near Alamein. When located, he was naked, save for a vest and one sock: he said he was 'waiting to be posted'.

'MONTY'

In 1941 a new power came on the scene. Montgomery! He was put in charge of Southern Command. He removed all the pink fat-faced, Huntin', Shootin' and Fishin' chota peg-swilling officers who were sittin' round waitin' to "see off the Bosche". To date we'd done very little Physical Training. We had done a sort of half hearted knees-up mother brown for five minutes in the morning, followed by conducted coughing, but that's all.

One morning a chill of horror ran through the serried ranks. There in Part Two Orders were the words: "At 06:00 hours the Battery will assemble for a FIVE MILE RUN!" Strong gunners fell fainting to the floor, some lay weeping on their beds. FIVE MILES? There was no such distance! FIVE MILES!?!? That wasn't a run, that was deportation! On that fateful dawn the duty Bombardier bade us rise: "Wakey Wakey, Hands off Cocks on Socks." The defenders of England rose wraith-like from their blankets. All silent, save those great lung-wracking coughs that follow early morning cigarettes. The cough would start in silence; first there was the great inhale, the smoke sucked deep down into the lungs, and held there while the victim started what was to be an agonised body spasm. The face would first turn sweaty lemon, the shoulders hunched, the back humped like Brahmin bull. The legs would bend, the hand grabbed the thighs to support the coming convulsion. The cough would start somewhere down in the shins, the eyes would be screwed tight to prevent being jettisoned from the head, the mouth gripped tight to preserve the teeth. Suddenly! from afar comes a rumbling like a hundred Early Victorian Water Closets. Slowly the body would start to tremble and the bones to rattle. The first things to shake were the ankles, then up the shins travelled the shakes, and next the knees would revolve and turn jelliform; from there up the thighs to the stomach it came, now heading for the blackened lungs. This was the stage when a sound like a three ton garden roller being pulled over corrugated iron was heard approaching the heaving chest. Following this up the convulsed body was a colour pattern, from a delicate green at the ankles to layers of pinks, blue, varicose purple, and sweaty red. As the cough rose up the inflated throat, the whole six colours were pushed up into the victim's face. It had now reached the inner mouth; the last line of defence, the cheeks, were blown out the size of football bladders. The climax was nigh! The whole body was now a purple shuddering mass! After several mammoth attempts to contain the cough, the mouth would finally explode open! Loose teeth would fly out, bits of breakfast, and a terrible rasping noise filled the room, Aweeioussheiough!!! followed by a long, silent stream of spume-laden air: on and on it went until the whole body was drained of oxygen, the eyes were popping, and veins like vines standing out on the head, which was now down 'twixt knees. This atrophied pose held for seconds. Finally, with a dying attempt, fresh air was sucked back into the body, just in time to do it all over again. Bear in mind this was usually performed by some sixty men all at the same time. Whenever I see those bronzed 'Jet Set Men' whose passport to International smoking is a King Size, I can't help but recall those Bronchial Dawn Coughing Wrecks.

So to the great run. Hundreds of white shivering things were paraded outside Worthingholm. Officers out of uniform seemed stripped of all authority. Lieutenant Walker looked very like a bank clerk who couldn't. Now I, like many others, had no intention of running five miles, oh, no. We would hang behind, fade into the background, find a quiet haystack, wait for the return and rejoin them. Montgomery had thought of that. We were all put on three ton trucks and driven FIVE MILES into the country and dropped. So it started. Some, already exhausted having to climb off the lorry, were begging for the *coup de grâce*. Off we went, Leather Suitcase in front: in ten seconds he was trailing at the back. "Rest," he cried, collapsing in a ditch. We rested five minutes and then he called, "Right, follow me." Ten seconds – he collapsed again. We left him expiring by the road.

Many tried to husband their energy by running on one leg. It was too cold to walk, we had to keep moving or hoar frost got at the appendages. One by one we arrived back at the billets, behind was a five mile train of broken men. It took two hours before the last of the stragglers arrived back. As a military disaster, the run was second only to Isandhlawana. It was the end of the line for Leather Suitcase.

Our new C.O. was Major Chaterjack, M.C., D.S.O. In the months that followed he ran us across two-thirds of Sussex, the whole of the South Coast, over mountains, through haystacks, along railway lines, up trees, down sewers, anywhere.

Major Chaterjack, M.C., D.S.O. (This photograph shows him in 1945 when he was a lieutenant-colonel)

If ever we had to retreat we were in tip top condition.

In the first week herds of men reported sick with sore feet. Busty Roberts told us the cure: "Piss in yer boots, lads, let 'em stand overnight." By God, it worked! There were accidents; forgetful sleepers got up and plunged their feet into boots full of cold urine. What an Army! What a life! I still can't believe it happened. But of course, the Russians were advancing on all fronts, the Yanks were coming, and we had our first case of Crabs. I had no idea what the crabs (or, as Smudge Smith said, 'Sandy McNabs') were. The victim was Sergeant Cusak – he discovered he got them on the eve of a week's leave. The M.O. told him to apply 'Blue Unction'. Now blue unction has only one use – to destroy crabs. Knowing this, Sergeant Cusak entered Boots in Piccadilly with a prescription during the rush hour on Friday – it was crowded. He whispered to the assistant, "Can I have some blue unction?" In a voice that could be heard up Regent Street the assistant said "BLUE UNCTION??" Cusak replied twice as loud, "YES, I'VE GOT BLOODY CRABS!"

BARRACK ROOM HUMOUR – JOKES – PRANKS

What I am about to relate is bawdy and vulgar but as it's true, it stands on its own merits.

It was after lights out that some of the most hysterical moments occurred. Those who had been drinking heavily soon made it known by great asphyxiating farts that rendered their owners unconscious and cleared the beds all round. There were even more gentlemen who performed feats with their unwanted nether winds that not even great Petomane could have eclipsed; simply, they set fire to them. The 'artiste' would bend down, his assistant stood by with a lighted match. When the 'artiste' let off, he ignited it. Using this method I have seen sheets of blue flame up to a foot in length. Old timers, by conserving their fuel, could scorch a Tudor Rose on the wall. There was Signaller 'X' whose control of the anal sphincter allowed him to pass morse code messages. With my own ears I heard him send S.O.S. On these occasions I, like others, lay in bed crying with laughter. But the most unbelievable 'act' was Gunner 'Plunger' Bailey, who did an entire twenty minute act with his genitals.

It was done on a very professional basis. After lights out a gunner would use a torch as a spot light, which lit the 'artiste's' genitals: the third member of the 'act', Bill Hall, sang 'Bird Song at Eventide' as the star manipulated his genitals to resemble 'Sausage on a Plate', 'The Last Turkey in the Shop', 'Sack of Flour', 'The Roaring of the Lions', and by using spectacles 'Groucho Marx'. Finally for the National Anthem he made the member stand. Each manipulation was received with a storm of clapping and cries of 'Encore'.

Snoring. Each one had his own unique sound. Gunner Forest's was like gargling with raw eggs through a gently revolving football rattle. For sheer noise, Gunner Notts. He vibrated knives, forks and spoons on the other side of the room. Before he went to sleep we secured all the loose objects with weights. Syd Price gave off snores so vibrant, his bed travelled up to six inches a night. On bad nights we'd find it out in the passage. Next, the teeth grinders! Gunner Leech's was like a dry cork twisting in the neck of a bottle, followed by the word, 'Fissss-ssshhhhhhh!'

This next story was passed on from A Sub-section, stationed at Alfriston. The gun crew were billeted in a beautiful old inn. The men were given the whole length of the attic. At one end was the Great Gun Bucket that gunners place in their midst for use in inclement weather. It was worth its weight in gold, but there were the 'spoilers'. These men, when the tub was full, would sneak up in the dark, and silently relieve themselves: this caused 'spillage', and gradually, without their knowledge, the floor and the ceiling underneath were starting to rot. Came the terrible night, when Lieutenant Sebag-Montefiore, sleeping soundly below was awakened by the sound of the ceiling falling through on him, followed by some twenty gallons of well-matured urine.

There was a hell of a row, the landlord demanded compensation, etc. The ceiling was made good, the Gunners reprimanded, and it all blew over, all except the smell. For months after – if you were down wind – you could always tell where Lieutenant Sebag-Montefiore was.

The Night of the Gun Bucket

MOVING TO MILL WOOD

1941: during which the sole stratagem of the Army in England was one of continual movement. They chose the most excruciating moments. After spending months making your billet comfortable came the order 'Prepare to Move'. This time I was just about to lay my new Axminster, when the order came. It was awful, I had to sell the piano. The moves were always highly secret and came in highly sealed envelopes, the contents of which usually appeared in later editions of the *Bexhill Observer*. Secrecy was impossible, enemy agents had only to

Shaving al fresco in Mill Wood, with the Germans only forty miles away. The cross eyes were the result of a blunt blade

follow the trail of illegitimate births. Another obsession was
'night occupation'. The swearing, the mighty oaths and clangs,
told the whole area exactly what was happening. It was quite
normal for a pub to empty out and give a hand pulling the gun.
Most kids in Bexhill could dismantle one. Our first move was
to a 'specially selected' muddy disused rubbish tip at Mill
Wood, two miles from Worthingholm. The signal section under
Sergeant Dawson had to start the lark of laying new lines.
This was simple: you went from Point A, the O.P., and took the
line to Point B, the Gun Position. Taking a rough bearing, we
set off carrying great revolving iron drums of D.5* telephone
cable. We had to cross railway lines, roads, swamps, rivers,
with no more than adhesive tape. We borrowed the equipment
en route from houses, a ladder here, a pair of pliers there, a bit
of string, a few hooks, a three course lunch, etc.

To cross roads we had to climb telegraph poles. Basically
lazy, it took some half an hour of arguing and threats to get

* I don't know what it means either

*Me, line laying. My tin hat had just fallen off and I was afraid
of dive-bombers*

one of us to go up. It was always little Flash Gordon, he didn't want to climb the poles, but we hit him until he did.

We had a new addition to the family, a military ten line telephone exchange. This saved a great amount of cable laying; it also connected up to the G.P.O. It was installed in a concrete air-raid shelter at the back of Worthingholm. In 1962 I took a sentimental journey back to Bexhill. The shelter was overgrown with brambles; I pushed down the stairs and by the light of a match I saw the original telephone cables still in place on the wall where the exchange used to be. There was still a label on one. In faded lettering it said, 'Galley Hill O.P.' in my handwriting. The place was full of ghosts – I had to get out. One of the pleasures of Duty Signaller was listening to officers talking to their females. When we got a 'hot' conversation we plugged it straight through to all those poor lonely soldiers at their O.P.'s and gun positions. It was good to have friends.

At the new position we were to live under canvas. "It's very simple," said Sergeant Dawson. He was talking about the erection of a marquee. "I've been camping a lot in my time, I'll show you." Thirty Signallers drove to the R.A.O.C. Depot at Reigate in a three-ton truck. We were shown a great piece of rolled canvas, six foot by ten foot by five foot. From it hung numerous lengths of trailing ropes. In picking the thing up it was impossible not to stand on them. We lifted. It must have weighed three to four hundredweight, and it all seemed to be on my side. It was but a few yards to the truck, but somehow we found it impossible to get there. The lump was moved in much the confused way that ants carry a twig; there was a fair bit of going round in a circle, three paces backward – a little bit sideways – then lots of going round and round again. Straining around the edge were about twenty gunners, while underneath, taking the weight on their heads were ten more. There was frequent swearing, unending strings of instructions, but progress, none. The far side of the lump had started to unfold, so the carriers on that side were lost to sight and carrying blind. The whole thing was becoming absurd. The

lump was coming to pieces as we continually trod on trailing ropes. Those on the outside were getting tired, and the lump was getting lower and lower as the men underneath wilted.

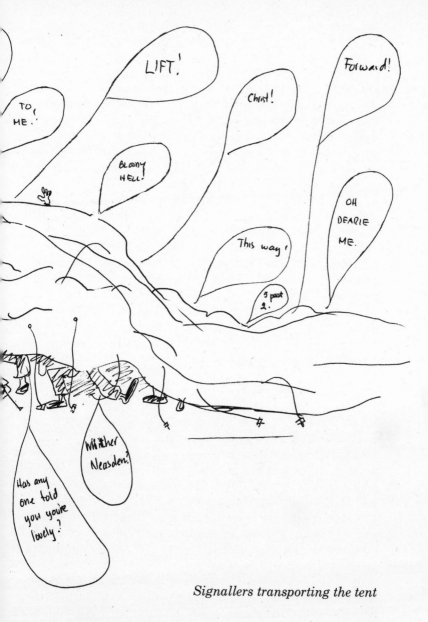

Signallers transporting the tent

Finally it collapsed with seventeen gunners underneath. The second attempt started. This time we just dragged the thing by its trailing edges and forced it into the lorry like stuffing a chicken. The lump now seemed much larger. We crawled on top of it and moved off. On arrival, we dragged what was now a long, uncontrolled canvas mess through the woods to the site. Sergeant Dawson was waiting. "What in the bloody hell have you done?" Bombardier Hart explained: "We fucked it up, Sarge." "We'll never win this bloody war," said Dawson as he circled the canvas monster. "Open it full length and try to fold it double on its side," he said. With a lot of twisting and un-twirling we finally got it like he wanted. "Now," he said, "where are the poles?" A hush fell on the multitude. "Poles, Sarge? Poles?" "Poles! . . . *Bloody Poles*!!!"

Ten of us were sent back for them. By careful planning we returned in time to finish work for the day. Next morning the nonsense continued. "First, three men take the head of the pole each, right, now *crawl* under the canvas towards where the roof is, right?" Muffled cries of "right". So far, so good. "Now, when you get to the roof seam we'll prod the outside where there is a hole for the pole to go in." Muffled Ayes. Underneath, the lumps, Gunners Gordon, Balfour and White, made their way to the holes. Two made it, but the third lump stayed still: it was Flash Gordon. "What's up now?" shouted Dawson. "I've dropped me money," said Flash. We stood idly by as the lump moved hither and thither. Finally Dawson, patience exhausted, said, "We can't wait, we're pulling the tent up, and you'll have to bloody well go with it." We were all given a rope each, eight men held the base of the two poles. "All together, heave." Marvellous! We got it up in one go, and had it down the other side on top of us. "You bloody idiots," yelled Sergeant Dawson. All the time Gunner Gordon's lump groped back and forth swearing the air blue. It came to the point when the marquee was at least standing upright, but covered in mud with a dozen gaping holes. Now came the tent pegs. The hammering in passed without incident. But some-thing looked wrong. Suddenly it dawned. "You stupid pricks," said Dawson. "The bloody thing's inside out!!" "Let's sleep on the outside," I suggested. He hit me. The whole lunatic job started again. By sundown the thing was up. Gunner White found Gordon's missing money. That night we all drank

78

Gunner Gordon's health. A mile away, in the dark, Gordon
on his hands and knees was searching the ground with a candle.

BURNING OF THE CLUBS (MILL WOOD)

It was during this time the Goons in the Popeye cartoon
appeared and tickled my sense of humour, and any soldier
I thought was an idiot I called a Goon. This was taken up by
those with a like sense of humour. We called ourselves the
Clubbers. We built a club rack outside the marquee and, in
time, we fashioned great gnarled clubs from fallen branches.
They all had names – "Nurkes Nut Nourisher", "Instant
Lumps". The pride was a magnificent find by Gunner Devine; it
was a part of a blasted oak, five feet long, almost a replica of the
club of Hercules. We added to it by driving earthing irons into
the head. It was solemnly christened, "Ye Crust Modifier". The
way the Clubbers were assembled was by a trumpet call based
on the Fanfare from the 'Boys from Syracuse' film. Immediately
the gang would do 'Hollywood Rhubards', rush forth, grab the
clubs, run into the woods hitting trees and shouting "Death to
the Goons". This exercise was our downfall. We were caught
one summer night by the duty officer. Drunk and naked, we
were running through the woods wielding clubs and yelling
"Viva Joe Stalin". We were ordered to destroy the weapons.
We had a solemn funeral procession. They would have to burn
in warrior's graves. These turned out to be the disused rubbish
tip at the bottom of a gently sloping hill. Rubbish was dumped
by trucks via a small gauge railway. Filling the truck with
clubs, we soaked them in petrol and set them ablaze. Giving
the truck a start we jumped on, Edgington in front, holding
on with his arms stretched backwards, looking like a ship's
figure head. The truck gathered momentum, flames built up,
we were gathering speed and singing "Round and round went
the bloody great wheel", when suddenly it occurred to me there
was no method of braking. As we careered towards a mountain
of old tins, crying with laughter, I shouted, "Jump for it". We
all leaped clear, save Edgington, who seemed transfixed. At

*Gunner Edgington about to make his famous last-minute leap
at Mill Wood Rubbish Tip from the flaming club truck*

the very last minute he let out a strangulated castrati scream
and hurled himself sideways as the blazing truck buried itself
into the mountain of tins with an ear splitting crash.

It was a fitting Viking end for the Sacred Clubs. Occasions of insanity such as this stopped us all going mad.

The Gun Position Telephone at Mill Wood was in a small wooden hut nine foot by eight foot, some two hundred yards from the gun. We were fairly isolated, off the road, in what had been a sand quarry. The hut backed on to the working face of a sandy cliff about fifteen feet high. Around and above grew gorse and brambles. It was a perfect get-away place, so much so that I used to volunteer to do any other signaller's duty. It was simple. You sat by the phone and every hour tested the line to Battery Exchange. Twice a day we'd take down something called a M.E.T. These were figures that I didn't understand, all to do with temperatures and barometric pressures. The G.P.O.A.* 'Specialists' would work out from a book of tables what effect this information had upon the fusing of the shells and ranging. It was all too much for me. A week's duty in the hut all centred around a gramophone lent by Nick Carter, and jazz records I would bring back from leave. Happiness was a mug of tea, a cigarette, and a record of Bunny Berrigan playing 'Let's do it'. Sharing it with a friend like Harry rounded off the occasion. What's happened to us all since then? The world's gone sour. Happiness is a yesterday thing.

Ablutions were primitive. We crossed the road into Bexhill Cemetery. By the grave of a 'Mrs K. Loughborough, died 23 September 1899. Not Dead just Sleeping' was a tap. That was it. There are few finer sights than a duty signaller scrubbing his dirty laundry on the marble slab of Mrs Loughborough's last resting place. " 'Not Dead just Sleeping'?" said Chalky White as he read her inscription. "She's not kidding anyone but her bloody self," he said as he wrung his socks out on her.

In the evenings after dark, one or two of our favourite birds would visit us and bring fish and chips; once in we bolted the door.

As the days of 1940 came to an end, Dunkirk was sliding into history. The war was spreading; there seemed very little in

* Gun Position Officer's Assistant

81

the way of victories, there were constant reversals in Lybia and Greece. On my birthday, April 16th, 1941, London had its worst raid yet. But cheering news – May 14th was the first anniversary of – wait for it – The Home Guard!

IN BILLETS AGAIN

After a winter under canvas it was good news that we were to be billeted in Turkey Road Girls' School. It was for us a paradise – large clean rooms – white walls, ideal for nails – parquet floors, a large ballroom, showers, a well-equipped gymnasium (which we pretended not to see) and finally a brand new upright piano, on which Harry could play the bloody awful Warsaw Concerto. From here we ran our own dances. Captain Martin registered 19 Battery as a Limited Company and sold shares to sister Regiments. At this new billet we received morning visits from a W.V.S. Canteen Van. A very dolly married woman took a fancy to me and one night, after a dance, she took me home. Strange aftermath: a week later I thumbed a lift to Eastbourne, a civvy car: inside I could smell her perfume.

"My wife works for the W.V.S.," said the driver.

"Really?" I said.

It was all sex in those days – it was that or the 'flicks' and flicks cost money. There was a lovely busty bird called Beryl, who had hot pants for me.

During the interval of our first dance at Turkey Road I took her to the lorry park, into the back of a fifteen hundredweight truck. We were going through our third encore when the truck drove off. Apart from the jolting it must have been the best ride we've ever had. It stopped at Hastings. Through the flap I saw our chauffeur was Sergeant 'Boner' Hughes who hated my guts (I don't know why, he'd never seen them). He backed the truck up an alley and left it while he went into The White Lion for a drink with his bird who was barmaid. Slipping into the driving seat I drove it back, and arrived in time to play the second half of the dance. "Where the bloody hell have you been?" asked Edgington, sweating at the piano. "I, Harry,

D Battery band playing at Turkey Road School, 1942

have been having it off in the back of a lorry, and I got carried away."

7.2 GUNS AND THE TIGER SCHEME

Our 9.2 guns were past it. Every time they fired, bits fell off. In place of bolts and nuts were bent nails and chicken wire. Gunners on leave would rummage through their sheds for screws, pinions, etc. The end came when elastic bands, which held the gun-sight together, were no longer obtainable. The Major wrote away, asking for a new gun for Christmas. One day they arrived. Dozens of them! 7.2 gun howitzers. Huge things towed behind Giant Schamell lorries.

At once we were put into vigorous training to familiarize us with the new toys. For weeks the area rang to the clang of breech-blocks, shouted orders, grunts of the sweating ammunition numbers. The guns threw a 280 pound projectile 17,800 yards, so you weren't safe any where except at 18,000 yards. Momentum was mounting, we were getting new field tele-

A 7·2 gun howitzer as seen from the receiving end

(The Imperial War Museum)

phones, wireless trucks, wireless sets, tommy guns, Tannoy loudspeakers that linked Command Post to the guns. The war effort was moving into top gear.

Monty sprang a giant Southern Command scheme, code name 'Tiger'. One autumn dawn the sky was a mass of grey sponges: this undoubtedly would be the day. It was. Off we went. One hour after off we went we stopped wenting. We were in the middle of a Rain Forest that appeared to be in the Mato Grosso.

"Dismount," came the waterlogged order. Soggy officers were called to the O.C.'s car. They stood in a squelching semi-circle, holding maps. Chaterjack whipped through the map references and all that Khaki Jazz. Our officer was Tony Goldsmith. "We've got to set up an O.P. at Map Reference 8975–4564* in half an hour. Synchronise watches." None of us had one. "Very well," said Goldsmith. "*I'll* synchronise watches." Goldsmith's map reading left something to be desired, like someone to read it for him. Using his method, we had arrived at a hundred-year-old deserted chalk quarry. How can people be so heartless as to desert a hundred-year-old chalk quarry? We were two hundred feet below sea level. We got out. Goldsmith consulted his map. "There must be something wrong," he said, looking intelligent at two hundred feet below sea level. "According to my calculations we should be on top of a hill, looking down a valley."

Gunner Milligan said, "But we aren't on top of a hill looking down a valley, are we sir?"

"No, we're not, Milligan. How shrewd of you to notice. This could mean promotion for you, or death. I suggest we retrace our steps to the main road. Does anybody know where it is?"

"I think I do sir," said Driver Wenham.

We boarded the truck, and set off somewhere. "Send a message to H.Q.," said Goldsmith, still trying to maintain the illusion of efficiency. "Say, 'Truck in ditch, will be late for O.P.'"

I sent off the message. But received a request for Goldsmith to speak to 'Sunray' (code name for C.O.). What a lovely name I thought for a dripping wet C.O.

Goldsmith spoke.

"Hello, Sunray, Seagull here. Over."

Chaterjack: Tony? What the bloody hell's going on? Over.

Goldsmith: The truck's stuck, sir. Over.

Chaterjack: Well hurry up, the whole bloody battery's waiting for you.

We drove grimly on. One o'clock. "Get the BBC news, Milligan," said Goldsmith, "you never know, it might be all

* Somewhere on the South Downs

85

over." There were the opening bars of Beethoven's Fifth Symphony. "I wonder if he gets royalties," said Goldsmith. "Oh yes," I said, "every Friday." The news. Russians were advancing on all fronts. Then a list of current British disasters, retreats, sinkings, etc. The news concluded with a report of a two-headed calf born in Hereford.

Using all the skill of a trained Army driver, Wenham had the truck into a ditch a second time!

"Sorry sir," said Wenham, "I won't do it again!"

"Don't stop now man, you're just getting the hang of it," said Goldsmith. "Milligan! Send another message. 'Truck now in second ditch.'"

Back came Chaterjack.

Chaterjack: Good God, Tony, where are you man? Over.

Goldsmith: About a mile from the O.P. sir. Over.

Chaterjack: You're very faint. Over.

Goldsmith: It's the food sir. Over.

Chaterjack: I can't hear you. Look, we'll have to write you off. We'll get 18 Battery O.P. to fire us. Over.

Goldsmith: Roger sir. Over.

Chaterjack: Anything else? Over.

Goldsmith: A two-headed calf has been born at Hereford sir. Over.

Chaterjack: Two what? Over.

Goldsmith: Very good sir, anything else?

Chaterjack: No. Roger and out.

We stopped at a village of Lower Lind, where we went to the Essoldo Bioscope Cinema to see 'Black Moonlight' with Anton Walbrook, and heard that bloody awful Warsaw Concerto. Lieutenant Goldsmith paid for us all, as is fitting for a man wearing the King's uniform over his Queen's College body.

He told me a story about Jesus College, Cambridge. It was Christmas morning, the phone rang in the gate porter's lodge. "Hello," said the porter.

"Is that Jesus?" asked a donnish voice.

"Yes."

The voice sang, "Happy birthday to you."

At six o'clock we arrived at the night rendezvous, a field of bracken resting on a lake. We got tea from a swearing cook-house crew, who took it in turns to say "piss off" to us. We were given to understand we could have a complete night's sleep. Good. We tossed for who was to sleep in the truck. I lost. Sod. Rain. Idea! Under the truck! Laid out ground sheet, rolled myself like a casserole in three blankets. I dropped into a deep sleep. I awoke to rain falling on me. The truck had gone. Everybody had gone. There had been a surprise call to action

I was alone in a fifty-acre field

at 02:00 hours. I was alone in a fifty-acre field. I shouted into the darkness, "Anybody there?" I was still alone in a fifty-acre field. Smell of oil – I felt my face. It was smothered. The stuff had dripped from a leaky sump. Sound of motor-bike approaching. "Help," I said. "Who's that?" said a voice. It was Jordy Dawson.

"It's me, Sarge! Milligan." A torch shone.

"What in Christ has happened to you?" he said.

"I'm doing Paul Robeson impressions. You're just in time for my encore." I started to sing: "Ole man ribber, dat ole . . ."

"What's that on your mush?"

"Oil, Sarge! I cut an artery and struck oil. We're rich, do you hear me. We can be married." He started to laugh. "You silly bugger, we've had half the bloody signal section looking for you. The scheme's over."

"I know! Half of it's over me," I said.

"Come on, I'll take you back."

"Go back?" I said in a pained voice, "but I'm happy here here on de ole plantation, massa baws." Seated on the pillion he drove me back to Bexhill. Tiger had been a roaring success. The German High Command must have been ecstatic. The following is an excerpt from the Regimental war diary of the time:

When the weather was too bad for schemes out of doors wireless and telephone exercises were held within the Regiment to increase the proficiency in communications. It was on such an occasion as this, that a message reading "Invasion Fleet in the Channel, two miles off SEAFORD steaming N.W. Estimated strength three capital ships, sixteen destroyers, and many lesser craft." He had omitted to prefix the message with the magic word "PRACTICE" and by some unkind trick of fate, which has never since been accounted for, the message by-passed R.H.Q. and was sent direct to Corps. The scheme finished, and the Regiment prepared to depart on its nightly occupations. Suddenly the peace was shattered by the frantic ringing of the telephone bell. It was a call from the War Office, who enquired in no uncertain tones, what the thundering blazes was the meaning of our message. What steps had been taken by us: and had the Navy been informed?

By the time that the matter had been sorted out, tempers were frayed and feeling was running high. It took some laughing off, but a personal visit by the C.O. to the War Office the following day succeeded in allaying the storm. It is an interview that few of us would have cared to undertake personally.

I think I can now safely reveal that the signal was sent by 954024, Gunner Milligan.

SPORTS

Invitations to join the Battery boxing team had fallen flat. We had one professional, Sergeant Conroy, but he wasn't going to do any boxing, oh no, he was, to quote him, going to "Pluck another Jimmy Wilde from our ranks." He plucked Lofty Andrews, a bean pole, six-foot-one, with a pigeon-chest. Conroy explained: "This lad is God's gift to me, he's as tall as a heavy-weight, with the same reach and he only weighs eight stone! Now boxers at that weight are usually only five-foot-six. Don't you see? With Lofty's reach, they won't get near him!"

But before that, the Battery were to have another champion. Southern Command Sports were coming up. One of our competitors was Gunner Alexander Naze who had entered for the high jump. This puzzled us. He was the most unathletic person I'd ever met. Such was his confidence, he never trained. Came the day and Bexhill Sports Ground was crammed with shouting soldiers and things. The weather was perfect, sunny, warm, with a delightful cool, salt-scented breeze from the Channel. The grass was a fresh cut green. How can people have wars! Among the contestants were professional athletes from pre-service days; some Canadian high jumpers were clearing the bar at five-foot-eight just as a warm up! To date, no sign of

Gunner Naze. Then we saw it. Issuing from under the stands was a figure. It was wearing a red hooped football jersey, elastic-waisted blue military P.T. shorts that reach just below the knee, grey army socks dangling round his ankles and white, slightly over-large plimsolls. He ran in a series of peculiar little bounds and leaps, flicking his feet behind him, which I thought was some sort of expertise muscle-loosening exercise. He was blissfully unaware of the comparison his comic garb made with his sleek-muscled professionally-clad opponents. By then he had arrived at the jump-off; the warming up had been terminated. The official had taken down the bar and temporarily rested it at the three foot level . . . Naze eyed it . . . He walked some hundred yards from the bar, then turned and started to run. It wasn't until he was half-way there we realised he intended to jump. He gathered a sort of lumbering momentum but never got faster . . . finally reaching his goal, he launched himself into a schoolboy 'double-your-legs-under-you' style jump and *just* managed to clear it. He seemed well pleased, unconscious of the puzzled look that followed his effort. Came time for the jump off. An official signalled Naze and asked him if he was competing. Naze nodded. Naze walked twenty yards away, turned, and now saw that the officials had set the bar at five foot. For the first time he looked worried. He walked back a further fifty yards. He started his approach. The stadium fell quiet as the great athlete bounded across the grass. We all felt that something unusual was about to happen. On and on he came, making little clenching gestures with his hands . . . he reached the bar and with a triumphant shout of "Hoi Hup la!" and an almighty effort he hurled himself upwards. The bar broke across his forehead. Cheering broke out from the stands. Gunner Naze kept running, he left the field, he left the stadium, he left athletics. Our next hope of a champion was the as yet untested Lofty Andrews.

*   *   *

*Gunner Naze about to commence his famous
jump*

The notice was pinned below the ticket office window in the
foyer of the De La Warr Pavillion. "Hurry-a-long, first fight
starts in minutes five – minutes five," said Sergeant Balcon in
his best voice. He was a strange-looking fellow, his eyes very
close together, his nose and ears so large they appeared to be
trying to outgrow each other. He spoke with that sound
peculiar to the cockney larynx, when it tries to speak posh. To
obtain this metallic sound, you press the chin down on to the
throat, applying slight pressure to the Adam's apple, you purse
the lips, the lower one slightly protruding, tense the tongue –
lay it flat in the well between the lower teeth and say "Yew".

Troops were rolling in; I sat thirteen rows back, between
Gunners Devine and White, Devine being no mean brawler
himself. "Why aren't you fightin' tonight, Devine?" asked
Captain Martin. "They won't let you use your head sir," said
Devine, going through the motion of nutting an opponent. The
hall was packed, and a great carillon of voices filled the ear.
Cigarette smoke wafted upwards from two thousand throats,
and hung like a pall in the still air. Old scores were being
settled with balls of paper flicked at the backs of unsuspecting
N.C.O.s' necks. Men were standing shouting to men in other
rows. Bombardier Rossi was taking bets in the tense region of
two shillings. The last of the officers were sauntering in,
flushed with hurried whiskies. They were greeted with cheers
or raspberries according to their popularity rating.

Now came guest of honour, Lieutenant-Colonel Harding. No
sooner had we all sat down, when came the National Anthem,
and very strangely. It was being played by Gunner Edgington
on a piano from the stage behind vast heavy velvet curtains
that acted as a baffle. As the first tinklings of the Anthem per-
meated the babble, it was a rare sight to see 2,000 soldiers in
various stages of patriotic uncertainty, those nearest could
hear and were at attention, those in the middle were somewhere
in between sitting and hovering in the half upright, while those

farthest away heard nothing and sat looking puzzled at the confusion around them.

"Wot's going on?"

"Stand up, it's the Nash-i-nole Anfem!"

"I can't 'ear it."

"It's behind the curtain!"

"What's behind the curtains?"

"The Nash-i-nole fuckin' Anfem!"

To try and weld the confused mass into one coherent whole, Colonel Harding started to sing "Send him vic-tor-rious, happy" etc., etc. He was joined by a few promotion-seeking officers. At the end, the small band of brave singers were given a tremendous ovation with shouts of encore enriched with farts. Edgington, thinking the applause was for him, appeared grinning through the curtain, a waste of time, as the house lights went off, blacking him out.

The ring now stood candescent in the floods, the light bouncing off the taut white ropes. Two miserable looking boxers sat in their corners, with towels draped over their shoulders. R.S.M. Warburton, scrubbed, gleaming in crisp S.D., tight at the neck, climbed into the canvas arena, his hair grease glistening in the lights, his brass buttons flashing. Referring to a card, he spoke in a voice like prodding bayonets, "Mi-Lords! Lay-dees! and gentlemen!!!" A voice from the dark shouts, "Go home, you Welsh bull shitter!" Warburton machine-guns the crowd with his eyes. "Gentlemen, please! The first fight on your programme is a fly-weight contest of three three-minutes rounds. At the weigh-in, Reynolds, in the red corner, weighed eight stone, two pounds!"

"Give the poor sod some grub!"

"Gentlemen, please!" This R.S.M. versus the rest continued until Warburton left the ring. The first three fights went through their thudding, sweating, grunting course – the animal in the crowd had been released, and tension lessened. Now came the bout we had come to see. "In the red corner, from D Battery, fifty six, fife-six-er Heavy Regiment Royal Artillery, Gunner Andrews." We cheered as Lofty stood. But the sight of his skinny body, with shoulder blades protruding from his back like wings, didn't look very promising. At the sight of him Bombardier Rossi's odds changed dramatically: he refused to take bets. In the opposite corner sat a red thing called Rifleman G. Motts. He was five-foot-six, covered in muscles, hair, scars, and tattoos of snakes disappearing into every orifice. Under neolithic brows, two evil black eyes stared out from hair which grew on his forehead. There was no neck, the head seemingly joined to the shoulders by the lobes of his ears. At the first sight of this creature Lofty tried to scramble out of the ring. "I'm not fightin' that until I 'ear it tork," said Lofty.

"Don't let appearances fool you," smoothed Conroy.

"They haven't," said Lofty.

"Seconds out, first round!"

The two grossly ill-matched contestants approach each other. The Bexhill air raid sirens went. Lofty, a nervous lad, immediately took cover lying face down on the canvas. The referee was puzzled. "You all right lad?" he said to the figure on the canvas.

"Yes."

"Then you'll have to stand up, or I'll start counting you out."

Lofty looked to Conroy for professional advice. He got it. "Get up you silly cunt." The remark was lost in the booing and jeering in true British sporting fashion. Lofty rose, the fight continued. Another disaster. The lights fused. More uproar and whistling. The lights went up. The referee was unconscious on the canvas. Lofty went to pick him up. Motts, seizing the opportunity, let go with a hay-maker that connected with Lofty's cheek and down he went. The bell went. Conroy dragged Lofty to his corner. R.S.M. Warburton dragged the referee out of the ring. The lights went out again. The bell for the second round. Someone in Motts's corner struck a match. The lights went on again. Lofty was still sitting on his stool and was crying.

"The rotten sod 'it me when I wasn't looking," he sobbed.

Conroy threw in the towel, and Lofty joined Naze in retirement. It wasn't the end. Lofty waited outside, and when Motts appeared, kicked him in the cobblers, then ran. I suppose you'd call it a draw.

Next, Rugby! Sergeant Griffiths fished around for players, rather, volunteers. In a hammer lock, I admitted I'd played stand-off for my Convent. Using threats he got together a scratch team. Our opponents were The Sussex Regiment. As they took the field, an uneasy feeling went through me. Each one was six foot and fourteen stone. It transpired that they were convicts who were given remission provided they joined the army. And now, *we* were going to pay for it. We won the toss but that's all. Griffiths kicked off. It was the last legitimate move of the game. From then on it was massacre. In the terrible scrums our hooker had his ears reduced to red flaps. In the rucks, our shins were kicked black. In the loose they tackled anyone, even each other. Their hand-offs were like walking into steel girders. The field rang to our screams. By half time, we were fifteen gibbering things, running white with fear and hiding on the crossbar. "Milligan! Come down at once you cowardly bugger," said Griff.

"They're not 'umen, Sarge," whined sixteen-stone Tiny Vickers, "I got a wife and kids to think of."

"Right, think of 'em while you're playing," said Griff.

The second half saw the end. In a moment of insanity, one of us had got the ball and was immediately crushed to the ground under six hundredweight of steaming beef. The brute I'd pounced on shot back his elbows, catching me flush under each eye. When I came to, I lay in a shallow, muddy grave. I looked up, play was at the far end and coming my way! "For Christ's sake don't get up!" screamed Griff, "or you'll put us all off side." I waited no more: I ran for my life, and hid under the stands.

I never played again. Nobody should. Rugby is for watching.

FEBRUARY 1941. MOVE FROM TURKEY ROAD SCHOOL TO HAILSHAM

One Sunday morning we Roman Catholics were religiously gathered around playing Pontoon. A devout Scots gunner was about to say "Pontoons Only" when Bombardier Bastard entered. "Stop," he said. The Scots gunner with a twenty-one hand, and therefore heir to a fortune, collapsed. Bastard spoke the well-known phrase: "Prepare to Move! Kit packed by 06:00 hours! Parade 06:15 hours! Full F.S.M.O.!" We were off again.

"Yes lads," said Bastard through clenched teeth, "we're all going tat-tars." He then detailed Edgington and myself to clean up the officers' billets at "Trevissick." "You will report back tue billets before 15:00 hours, understan'?" We understan'. We put on our denims and with two brooms grumbled our way to "Trevissick", a house in the posh area of Bexhill known as The Highlands. We picked up bits of paper, rusty blades, a sock, a broken record of Al Bowley singing 'Buddy can you spare a dime?'. "He's broke," I punned. We burnt all the rubbish and the brooms, then! a bit of Ould Oirish Luck. There in the corner of the garage was a crate of certain bottles. We drew nigh, and lo! there were two full bottles of liquid. One marked Barbados Rum, and the other, Soda Water. Being of a patriotic mien I volunteered to taste the rum in case it was poisoned. "I can't let you take all the risk," said Harry, "I must drink my share." The tasting went on for quite a while. Also being of a scientific mind, from time to time we mixed the soda with the rum. We gave of our best for over an hour. At 12:00 hours we were wandering, drinking, giggling, somewhere in Mill Wood. I challenged Edgington to a tree-climbing race. He said I couldn't climb a tree for toffee. I said, "Who climbs trees for toffee? I get mine in a shop."

At 13:00 hours we were still wandering, drinking and giggling, in a tree in Mill Wood. I said I could leap from the tree and say 'My Mum's Monkey Makes Many Mistakes' before I hit the ground. He said, Rubbish, I'd never get further than Mum's Monkey, but he could. I jumped but forgot to say it. He said it but forgot to jump, so he jumped while I said it.

The sun was setting, and an early crescent moon sailed towards the evening sky. Gunner Edgington lay on his back, looking up the neck of an empty rum bottle. "All gone," he said. "Gone, all gone," I said from the same position. We both stood up. He saluted, and fell down. I did an imitation of 'Last Post' over his recumbent body. "England's a beautiful country," he said and was sick. I don't know how, but we ended up at the house of a Lady Friend, a pretty girl with hairy legs, who was getting married next week. We sat and listened to her play Chopin. I sang "Chopin, I love you, you know I always will, I love most of your Nocturnes, and I'll sing them till I'm ill."

"Lovely," said Edgington, "Lovely."

We arrived back at Turkey Road in the dying moments of the Battery's departure. Great activity. We hoisted long under-wear up on the flagpole. We joined a queue going into the Q Stores, and came out with a case of prunes each. A duty Bomb-ardier, insane with military rage, put us under arrest for being late, drunk, improperly dressed, cheeking an N.C.O., bad language, the murder of Rasputin, and singing the Warsaw Concerto. "Get your kit into that fucking truck!" Piling on to that fucking truck, we drove into the night towards yet an-other secret destination. We lay on heaps of military gunge and sang the worst American song titles we could dream up: 'Galloping hooves in the night remind me I married a Centaur'; 'Little Dutch time bomb, tick-tock-Boom'; 'I'll wait for you till the end of time and then apply for an extension'. We were whistling the Warsaw Concerto when the lorry stopped. We'd arrived!

In the dark Harry and I unloaded our kit. The lorry drove away. He'd only stopped for a leak. We stood on the verge swearing. We sat on the verge swearing, which is the same as standing only lower down. We put our groundsheets down, covered up with blankets and went to sleep swearing. In the wee hours the truck returned. "You silly buggers," said the driver, "what did you get off for?" "Excitement," said Harry.

An hour later, we were dumped in the yard of a requisitioned livery stable cum dog breeders' kennels at the junction of the A295 and A22 (Hailsham–Eastbourne road). "Up in t'loft, that's where t'lads are sleeping," said the duty Bombardier. We climbed up and were met with the steamy fug that goes with sleeping gunners.

It was 5.30 a.m., no point in sleeping. We started to change into dry clothes; a perfect end to the whole night was nigh. I fell through a trap door. Edgington looked down from above.

"Cheer up," he said. "Remember, man with death-watch beetle in wooden leg better off than man with tin leg in thunderstorm." I made a certain gesture.

Our new H.Q. was Hailsham. In the town centre, an old Vicarage was commandeered as Battery Office; it was a maze of unending passages and dark brown rooms. I remember Lieutenant Walker, drunk, at two one morning, blundering through the darkened corridors shouting "Ariadne! the thread! The thread!"

Normal day. Reveille 06:30. Roll call, 07:00. Breakfast, 07:15. Parade, 08:00. Then training. Morse Code, Heliograph, Wireless, Jokes, Tea. Break at 10:30, when a N.A.F.F.I. Van arrived. Parade 11:00. More training. I was the clown of the Battery – I would give a demonstration of how to do rifle drill in Braille, how to sleep standing up on guard, how to teach a battledress to beg, how to march standing still.

Roll call one morning.

"Neat?"

"Sah!"

"Edgington?"

"Sah!"

"Milligan . . . MILLIGAN? . . . GUNNER MILLIGAN?"

"Sah!"

"Why didn't you answer the first time?"

"I thought I'd bring a little tension into your life, Sarge."

"Oh – well here's a little tension for you. TEN – SHUN! To cook house for fat-i-gues – Double!!"

FIGHT AT ROBIN'S POST – IN HAILSHAM

The Battery telephone exchange was in the grounds of Robin's Post, a private home on the A22 road between Horsefield and Polegate. Again it was an air-raid shelter but brand new, with shelves, wall beds, ventilation and plenty of electric points and lights. We were well away from everybody. Occasionally we'd get a visit from Lieutenant Goldsmith. During spells of duty we would make up what I suppose were the first dim adumbrations of the Goon Show. Here is a fragment of Harry Edgington's writings of that time:

> The door flew open and in crashed the master-spy himself, Gruenthaphartz, measuring five rounds gun-fire by inches three, and clad only in a huge fur coat of huge fur, a sou'-wester, and two hand-painted barges strapped to his feet for a quick getaway. With a hairy on the knee. He was escorted by a plague of Zeppelins. He loped across the room with a great lope and snatching up a sharpened lamp-post hurled it wildly at the bedraggled portrait of Sir Bennispon-of-du-Whacka. 'So perish all my enemies' he roared, and then, 'I have quoth,' whereupon they all leapt into a handy bus and drove off smiling and waving through the wildly cheering populace.
> "A near thing," he said, reaching for the wine, "that lamp-post must have been seven and one tooth."
> Curtain, to chord in various flats by orch. of military bugle, violin and Pianist who has one hand out to show he is going to turn right.

We wrote reams of this stuff. We read some to Lieutenant Goldsmith. "Very good," he said, moving in the general direction of away.

The Signal Section was a law unto itself. We organized the duty roster to suit ourselves. We all opted for one week's duty and one off. Two of you would work out who slept and kept awake. During the off week your presence in bed at midday was explained thus: "This man has been on duty all night, sir." It was all right having a whole week off, but it became boring. A sleeping contest was inaugurated. The rules were: 'The contestant will at no time leave the bed. The first to do so is disqualified.' So started the great sleep. Piddles were done out of the back window at night, standing on your bed. Food was hauled up in a kit bag when the N.A.A.F.I. van called at 10.30 of a morning. Tea was brought in by bribing Janker wallahs. The contestants were the Gunners Milligan, Edgington, White and Devine. There we lay for five days and nights. Sometimes we sang songs, told jokes, recounted past incidents.

"You know what I'd like to do to Bombardier Jones?"

"What?"

"Tie him to a post, then shoot him with a blunderbuss loaded with his own Shite."

"When I leave the army I'm not going to do anything for a year."

"You know what I'd like now? Four fried eggs, chips, bacon and tomatoes."

"Too many eggs give you the horn."

"I think this war will die out."

"Die out? How do you mean?"

"Well, stop. I mean everyone will get fed up. I'm fed up already."

"So am I. Let's all fuck off."

"Lend us a fag."

"You're always scroungin' bloody fags. What do you do with them?"

"I smoke 'em."

Edgington won the contest with six days and seven hours.

"Christ, how did you do it?" said Devine.

"Training," said Edgington, "that, and dreams of grandeur!"

About now the owner of the livery stables (retired livery Colonel) gave a dance for officers from local British and Canadian units; we were detailed to play.

British officers are possibly the world's worst ballroom dancers. One or two of the more daring ones would wag one finger in the air as they went 'Trucking'. First signs of repressed inhibitions came in the 'Paul Jones'. As they circled the ladies, there would be a few jolly Scottish whoops. Next they would do their 'Cocking of the Legs' which I will describe later.

The dance was held in a large and comfortable country-style lounge; chairs and sofas clad in loose floral covers, plenty of polished wood, a few Hercules Brabizon-Brabizon water colours on walls, standard lamps with silk shades, a few oriental curios, traces of visits to foreign climes. (What *are* foreign climes? Waiter! A pound of foreign climes, please!) As the

100

guests eased themselves in, we were playing lively tunes –
'Woodchopper's Ball', 'Don't sit under the apple tree', 'Ma, I
miss your apple pie', 'Honeysuckle Rose', 'Undecided', 'Tan-
gerine' (what memories these tunes bring back). Soon the floor
was crowded, drinks for the band were arriving at a steady
rate. Major Chaterjack, M.C., D.S.O., came over to see that we
were being 'looked after'; he was really a great soldier, I for
one would have followed him anywhere, preferably away from
the war. He was this kind of man. Autumn morning – the early
sun had melted the night frost, leaving glistening damp trees.
Battery parading – small wafts of steam are appearing from
men's mouths and noses – the muster roll is called – B.S.M. is
about to report to Major Chaterjack: 'Battery all correct and
present, sir!' The roar of a plane mixed with cannon shells all
over the place – M.E. 109 roof top, red propellor boss – panic –
Battery as one man into ditch – not Major Chaterjack, M.C.,
D.S.O. – stands alone in the road – unmoved – produces a
silver case, lights up a cigarette. He is smoking luxuriously as
we all sheepishly rise from what now feels like the gutter. He
addresses us: 'Very good – you realise you did the right thing
and I the wrong.' What can you say to a bloke like that?

Interval. We ditch our instruments and wander into the garden for a leak; finding a bush, we 'ease springs'; these were
accompanied by the usual postern blasts, each one greeted
with cries of "Good luck!" "Fall out the Officers!" "Drink up!
mine's a Guinness!" As eyes became accustomed to the dark,
I was horrified! five feet from us, on a garden seat, was Lieutenant Goldsmith and a bird. As we slunk away, he called out,
"Thank you gentlemen, and what time is the next perform-
ance?" This was too much, we broke out into uncontrollable
laughter and once started, we couldn't stop. By the time we got
to the house, I was holding my sides with pain. On entering we
saw a huge fat woman, seated at the drums, making a bloody
fool of herself. This finished me off. The dance restarted.

Without warning, a Canadian officer poured a beer into the
bell of my saxophone – (Yes! I also played that) – which he
thought funny. I threw the contents on to his jacket, something
he didn't think funny. He grabbed the saxophone. I stopped

101

playing. "Let go," I said, "this is a solo instrument." Our host came over. The Canadian was told that it "wasn't the done thing." The dance continued and we, rather *I*, got drunker. Time now for what I told you was the 'Leg Cocking'; this is an English officer gyration. The man assumes the position for a Highland Reel, and then at the sound of 2/4 or 6/8 tempo, he raises his right leg and leaps all over the room with one hand up in the air and one on his hip. We played 'Highland Laddie'; at once the floor became a mass of leaping twits all yelling "Och! Aye!" This is where the fight started. One of the batmen serving drinks had his tray knocked flying all over a Mrs Hendricks. Captain Hendricks hit someone, someone else hit him. This became popular. The room became a mêlée of fisti-cuffs and gentlemen. "Somebody stop them," shrieked Mrs Hendricks, as someone floored her. Our host rushed up: "Quick, play a waltz." We launched into 'Moonlight Madonna'. Someone hit Major Chaterjack, M.C., D.S.O. His batman laid out the offender, then carried Chaterjack, M.C., D.S.O. to safety. To help it all along, Doug Kidgell threw an occasional cream cake into the arena. The addition of confectionery to the struggling mass made exotic pictures. A red-faced major, his bald head supporting a chocolate éclair, hit a Canadian sport-ing a jam-covered ear. Kidgell's masterpiece: a large circular cream-topped cake that stuck to the back of a long officer's head. For moments he stood like Greco's Christ Ascending until a loping right felled him. The cake was picked up by a foot, which trod it all over a chest, that passed it on to a neck. In a short time, cream, jam, and treacle, were liberally dis-tributed on the uniforms of His Majesty's Officers. Strawberry flan up the front of the jacket, apple strudel on the lower face, plus little blobs of cream on the epaulettes was something we found difficult to salute. Someone covered in lemon-curd was hit backwards through an open window. Our host, his head split open, suddenly appeared, rising cross-eyed and smiling above the mass. "Molly," he shouted and disappeared again. The news from Moscow was good. Major Chaterjack, M.C., D.S.O. had recovered enough to come on again and was ren-dered unconscious for the second time. He was immediately trodden underfoot. His batman grabbed his ankles and pulled him from the carnage, a seraphic smile on his face. There seemed no sign of the fight abating, so we played 'God save the King', and packed our gear. There was a lot of booze left in the kitchen. We drank it. Legend has it I slid to the floor, first calling for my mother or a priest. To make matters worse, the band truck wouldn't start, so Edgington and Fildes dragged me along between them, with Kidgell walking behind making remarks. The billet was a mile and a half away, but after a while

The Great Fight at Robin's Post

the Gunners Edgington and Fildes dropped Gunner Milligan in a ditch and said, "Sod it." They sat a while smoking and Driver Kidgell said, "I'll go and 'phone for a truck." An hour later the water waggon arrived. It was two in the morning and I was starting to surface enough to notice that all the dragging had removed the soles from my boots. There was only enough room for three in the cabin, so Edgington and I sat astride the water tank on the back and drove through the black silent streets of Hailsham shouting 'Night Soil'. Thank God there wasn't any.

Hailsham was this sort of place. If you look at it on the map, it's not marked. We made friends with a young Jazz drummer named Dixie Dean. His father owned a radio shop in Hailsham High Street.* Sunday evenings he'd invite the band to his room (over the shop), and we'd sit listening to records. I brought my records from home, and the Sunday night record session was something we looked forward to with great pleasure. Dixie's mother would come in at intervals with tea and cakes. When the regiment went overseas, I left my records with Dixie. "I'll collect them after the war" was my parting line. I did, but alas, the house had been hit in a raid, and among the losses was my record collection, all save one, which I still have – Jimmy Luncefords Bugs Parade. I daren't play it much; it creates such vivid memories. I have to go out for a walk; even then it's about three hours before I can settle down again.

During our stay at Hailsham a Captain John Counsell was posted to us. In those days I knew nothing about the theatre at all, so it was not until after the war I realised his connection with the Theatre Royal, Windsor. For the record I quote from his book, *Counsell's Opinion:*

> Thus, I found myself promoted to Captain it is true, but as second in command of D Battery, stationed at Bexhill and later at Hailsham.

* He's still there

104

I was with it five months, during which time we had three different Battery Commanders, between the first and second of which I had several weeks in temporary command. I greatly enjoyed this short burst of authority, when I could run things more or less my own way. I tried out one idea which seemed to me to be valuable – a public meeting of all ranks which followed the Saturday morning inspection. At it, anyone could make criticisms or suggestions to improve our standards of military proficiency or domestic arrangements. In deliberate contrast to the relaxed atmosphere of the public meetings, the inspection that preceded it was tough, rigorous and exacting. There was only one point in my tour where I used to detect a whiff of indiscipline. My exit from the O.P. was invariably followed by a roar of laughter. Someone had obviously cracked a quip at my expense, and I had no doubt who it was. To me he was known as 'Signaller Milligan' – to his mates simply 'Spike'. Years afterwards when my daughters submitted their autograph books to the Goons, one page was inscribed: 'To my old Captain's daughter – Spike Milligan.'

The only 'happening' in Hailsham was the Saturday dance in the Corn Exchange. Somehow we picked up a clarinet player, Sergeant Amstell. He was from the Heavy Coastal Artillery. This was a huge twelve-inch cannon mounted on a railway bogey with eight wheels and pulled by an engine. It was shunted back and forth along the South Coast wherever the German Invasion threatened. The gun crew lived in a converted railway carriage. The things they did! Late night, if they were short of fags, they'd actually drive the whole train, gun and all, to Hailsham Station, nip into The George, a quick pint, ten Woodbines, then back again. When Sergeant Amstell played with us at the Corn Exchange he'd drive the train three miles to Hailsham, park it at the station siding for the evening, then drive it back after the dance. Ridiculous!

Now, whereas wartime Hailsham offered boredom of an evening, nearby Eastbourne offered a greater variety of it. As a local said "There's nothing wrong with Hailsham, there's always the streets." On nights off Harry and I would thumb a lift to Eastbourne. As empty vehicle after empty vehicle went by we realised what a lot of bastards people were. A Canadian truck approached. When I saw it was not going to stop I waved it farewell. Immediately the truck stopped, backed up, and out jumped a furious noisy-voiced Canadian officer. He was incensed that I dared wave the truck farewell, "I'm not having any two bit private being a smart alec at my expense."

"Oh there's no expense sir," I said, "I did it free."

"It's forbidden for military vehicles to stop to give anyone a lift." Having had his moment of power he drove away, taking his tiny mind with him. What can you say or do to a person like that? I mean, I was wishing he'd get killed the first day in action. My God, he started a chain reaction – from then on I never gave any Canadian officer a lift, ever. Aren't I a swine? (Heh-heh-heh-heh.)

Our first visit to Eastbourne led us to a pub from which issued forth music. The customers were all squaddies and their girls. The music was supplied by three elderly gentlemen on a small rostrum. Piano, violin and cello. They made desperate attempts to be 'with it' by playing 'In the Mood', 'Beat me daddy eight to the Bar' etc., but one felt that death was nigh. Suddenly, in the middle of a tune, the violinist downed his violin, started to collect the empty glasses which he took to the bar.

"What an original arrangement," said Harry. "Sixteen bars solo, then eight bars collecting empties. This could open up a whole new field of entertainment." I agreed. "What's wrong with sixteen bars solo, then eight bars painting the landing, and another eight bars chopping wood. Great."

Harry spotted it. The fiddle player only got down to collect the empties when the tune went into more than three flats. We spent the rest of the evening listening for the key changes; "This is it, he'll start collecting 'em now," said Harry gleefully, as the maestro did exactly that.

Ever on the search for money, we asked the landlord if he'd like us to play some Jazz one evening. He was a tall, very fat

Florrie, the landlady at the Eastbourne pub we played at in 1942, as I remember her

man. His face so red it appeared to have been sandpapered. He liked the idea but, "I'll have to speak to the Missus. Florrie!" Florrie arrived from the dark recesses of the saloon bar. "Jazz?" she said, "isn't that the noisy stuff?" We assured her that it wasn't. It was finally agreed we would be given a try-out the coming Saturday. There was no money, but we could have drinks on the house, and we didn't have to collect the empties. It was nearly the last Saturday of my life.

Eastbourne and excitement are foreign to each other. Peacetime Eastbourne with its frail old ladies or russet-faced gentlemen dozing in wicker bath-chairs varied little from wartime. The town had been evacuated. The great wedding-cake hotels were boarded up or occupied by the Services. A few diehards remained. You'd see them mornings, sitting in bus shelters reading *The Times*, or ladies in deck chairs knitting Balaclavas. "Which war are we knitting for, Penelope?" They all objected to the triple skeins of barbed wire that ran the length of the sea-front disappearing towards Bexhill and Beachy Head. Who in their right mind would want to attack Eastbourne? It would get the town a bad name. They were still trying to live down the fact that Van Gogh once stayed there. I mean, trying to chop your ear off. It wasn't good enough.

Saturday night saw D Battery band swinging away there. The pub was really full, people passing heard the Jazz, and of course came in. The landlord was delighted. Never had such a crowd. People were standing jammed against the walls. The original trio were fully employed collecting the empties and looked much happier doing it, especially the violinist, whose name I discovered was *Percy Ants!* We *had* to play it, 'I can't dance, I've got ants in my pants'. Bang. Bang. Bang. Three shots rang out, a woman screamed. Bang. The wall mirror behind me shattered. There was a struggle going on in the entrance door. More women screamed (it might have been men but I didn't have time to check). Bang again, and I hear a projectile whizz past me and thud into the wall behind. It was a Scottish Tank Gunner, who had been thrown out because of offensive behaviour. Outside he drew his pistol and fired through the door. He had tried to get in, but a French Canadian soldier grabbed his pistol arm, and was now holding it pointed to the ceiling. This all happened in a flash. Recalling the heroism of the ship's orchestra on the *Titanic*, I went on playing. Turning round, I discovered that neither Edgington, Fildes nor Kidgell had heard of the *Titanic* affair and had gone. Kidgell had dived through a door that just happened to be marked 'Ladies'. There were understandable screams from the occupants within. Edgington and Fildes had rushed to the bar and demanded free drinks. The offending soldier was finally disarmed; the Military Police arrived and took him away.

Out of the 'Ladies' ran several females in various states of undress, followed sheepishly by Doug Kidgell. Things settled down, and we went on playing, but this time much quieter. If anything more was coming, we wanted to hear it. I visited the pub about three years ago. The place had been tarted up and Watneyised. The old landlord was gone. No one remembered him, nor the gunfight. The rostrum and the old piano were there. I went over and touched the keyboard. It was like patting an old horse you once knew.

LARKHILL

Things had been going too smoothly to continue as they were, it really was time we had another bout of applied chaos. It came in the shape of a sudden rush to Larkhill Artillery Camp, Salisbury, hard by Stonehenge. It was January 1942, and quite the bitterest weather I could remember. We arrived after a Dawn to Sunset trip by road. Salisbury Plain was blue-white with hoar-frost. I sat in the back of a Humber Radio Car, listening to any music I could pick up from the BBC and banging my feet to keep warm. We arrived tired, but being young and tired means you could go on all night! Ha! Having parked the vehicles, we were dismissed. The signallers were shown to a long wooded hut on brick piers. We dumped our kit on the beds, with the usual fight for the lower bunk, then made for the O.R.'s mess and began queueing. It must have been the season for schemes, as the whole place was swarming with gunners. We were given pale sausages, not long for this world, and potatoes so watery we drank them. The camp had masses of hot showers and we spent a pleasant hour under them, singing and enjoying the luxury of hot water. There were the usual comments about the size of one's 'wedding tackle': 'Cor, wot a beauty', or 'he's bloody well hung', or 'Christ, his poor wife', etc. After a quick tea and wad in the N.A.A.F.I. we went to the large cinema Nissen hut. It was The Glen Miller Orchestra in 'Sun Valley Serenade', and it was a feast of great Big band sound plus at least ten good songs. Sitting in the N.A.A.F.I. later, we tried to recall them; it was this way that we learnt most of the tunes for the band's repertoire. Seated at the piano, Harry tried to play some of the tunes from the film.

"Play Warsaw Concerto," said a drunk Scottish voice.

At dawn the next day the Battery set off on the great, ice-cold, frost-hardened Salisbury Plain. Most of us had put on two sets of woollen underwear, including the dreaded 'Long Johns'. We were to practise a new speedy method of bringing a twenty-five pounder gun into action. Ahead of us would go a scouting O.P.; somewhere on the Plain four twenty-five pounders drawn by quads would be moving in the direction of a

109

common map reference, all linked to the O.P. by wireless. Ahead the O.P. would establish itself at a point overlooking the enemy. Immediately, the O.P. would send out the signal 'Crash Action East', or whichever compass point applied; the information was received by the gun wireless, whose operator would shout out to the gun officer the order received. The gun officer, standing up in his truck would shout to the gun crew, 'Halt, Action East'. The quad would brake sharply, the gun crew in a frenzy unlimber the gun, and face it east; while they were doing this the O.P. would rapidly send down the Rough Range of the Target. As soon as the gun crew had done this, they fired. In our case, from the first order to the firing of the first round was twenty-five seconds. This was the fastest time for the day.

That night, in high spirits, we of the signal section decided to raid the specialists. After lights out some fifteen of us, faces blacked up, wearing balaclavas, carrying buckets of water and mud mixed to a delightful consistency, crept towards the specialists' hut. I remember being first in. In the ensuing fight I was mistaken for a specialist and got a bucket all to myself. For the

Larkhill: Crash Action Winners

next two hours there was a game of hide-and-seek among the huts as the specialists under Bombardier Aubery sought revenge. It was just too bad about Lieutenant Hughes, sitting quietly in the dark of the officers' toilet – he got a bucket of mud full face.

The next ten days saw us going through rigorous training. The weather was bitterly cold. I saw Sid Price smoke a cigarette down to the stub, and burn the woollen mitten on his hand without feeling a thing. On the last day, B Subsection were firing smoke shells, when one got jammed in the breech. Sergeant Jordy Rowlands was in the process of removing the charge when it exploded in his hand. When the smoke cleared Rowlands was looking at the stump of his wrist with his right hand ten yards away on the ground. There was a stunned silence and then he said, "Well, I'll be fooked." Apart from initial shock he was o.k., but for him the war finished on Salisbury Plain. The severed hand was buried where it fell by Busty Roberts. As he dug a small hole Driver Watts said, "You going to shake hands before you bury it?" Busty's reply was never recorded.

That night there was an Officers' and All-Ranks' dance in the Drill Hall. We all worked hard to extricate all the best-looking A.T.S. girls from the magnetic pull of the officers and sergeants. Alas, we failed, so we reverted to the time honoured sanctuary of the working man – Drink. We finally reached the stage of inebriation when we were willing to do the last dance with any good-looking Lance Bombardier. Next day, Saturday, the last day at Camp, we were allowed into Salisbury. I went to see the Cathedral. I'll never forget the feeling of awe when I walked in. A boys' choir was singing something that sounded like Monteverdi. The voices soared up to the fluted vaults as though on wings. The morning autumn sun was driving through the stained-glass windows throwing colours on to the floor of the nave, the whole building was a psalm in stone. It all made me aware of the indescribable joy derived from beauty. "Cor, it's bloody big, ain' it?" said Smudger Smith. He was right. It was bloody big.

There was a beer-up that night, and another dance. After

111

23:43 hours I don't remember anything. Next day we returned to that jewel of the south coast, Bexhill.

LEARNING TO DRIVE

The time had come, the Army said, to speak of many things, like teaching us to drive military vehicles; the reason was, we had new vehicles arriving at such a rate they were outnumbering the drivers; so, several of the Signal were selected for tuition, among them yours truly.

It was done under the supervision of Bombardier Ginger Edwards. It was not unpleasant. Every morning the trainees would be bundled in the back of a fifteen hundredweight Bedford truck and driven to a deserted country road, and instructions started from there. Allowing for the possible stupidity of the pupils the instructions were shot through with insults. The spelling is based on Bombardier Edwards's enunciation. "This end is the front end, the back is the arse end. This round object mounted on a spindle with three spokes is the steering wheel. Any questions? No? Good. Now this vehicle is like a human being, it has ter be fee-ed the right ingredients for it to go. Understand? The ingredients are One, Pet-er-ol, Hoil and Water, each one 'as its own hole for pourin' in, if you put it in the wrong 'ole it will cease to function," and so on. After the technical briefing we were each given a go at starting the engine and proceeding in first gear. Most of us got the hang of it very soon, all save Gunner Edgington; he managed to perform mechanical feats with the truck that were just impossible, i.e., Edgington at the wheel, truck ascending a steep gradient, Bombardier Edwards says, 'Now go down to first.' Edgington disengages from fourth and some how goes into reverse, but so smoothly, it was not until we had travelled backwards ten yards that the mistake was discovered. I myself had a moment of fear. We were approaching a T junction. "Turn left here," said Edwards. I did, but it was a trick, the road ended almost immediately in a rough field and it was intended to test my braking ability. I jammed my foot on to the brake, missed it and

112

went on to the accelerator, the truck shot forward down a two foot ditch; as we hit the field I pulled the wheel to the left to get us back on to the road, but for love nor money I could not get my foot off the accelerator. I just prayed. All the time there were yells and threats from the bouncing occupants on the back of the truck.

Finally after fifteen nightmare seconds, we hit the road again, where I managed to put my foot on the brake. There was dead silence then Edwards and I looked at each other and burst out laughing.

Another memorable moment was again Harry Edgington. Driving along the front at Hastings, Bombardier Edwards decided to test Edgington's reflexes. "Quick, stop, there's a child in the road," he shouts. "No there isn't," said Gunner Edgington.

From motor vehicles we went on to Bren Carriers, they were marvellous, they'd go anywhere, and didn't we just do that. Having passed all the tests, we were promoted to Driver Operators, which meant as from 24–10–42 I was a Class Three Tradesman Driver/Operator, so I got a few shillings more per day.

JANKERS

Jankers can be painful. It usually means confined to barracks and menial tasks like, "Soldier! Pick up that menial cigarette-end." My first jankers was for causing a fire. In the hard winter of 1940, coal fires were forbidden except on Sundays. But I was freezing on a Saturday. My bed was on the first floor, directly in line with the North Pole. The window was over the coal shed. With some rope and a length of bucket it was simple; Edgington went down, filled it, and I'd haul up. Suddenly, with a full bucket ascending, a snap inspection! "Orderly Officer! Eyes Front!" (Where else?) I turned, managed to face him, arms behind me. I nearly got away with it, but Edgington gave a tug on the rope to haul up, and I was pulled backwards out of the window. The game was up. I blamed Edgington. Edgington blamed me. We blamed the Germans, Florrie Ford and finally the Warsaw Concerto. Captain Martin gave us a roasting: "It's a degrading trick depriving other men of their fuel ration! Indeed, it's a disgrace!" he said, standing with his back to a roaring coal fire on a Monday. Most jankers time was spent lagging the plumbing; this was called 'up yer pipe'; another fatigue was peeling spuds. We delighted in peeling spuds to the size of peas. It made no difference, they cooked the peel as well.

It's not too difficult to become a military criminal. Not shaving, dirty boots, calling a sergeant "darling", or selling your Bren Carrier. Any Sunday, down Petticoat Lane, you could find some of the lads selling lorries, jerrycans, bullets, webbing. "Git your luverly Anti-Aircraft Guns 'ere." It got so that Military Depots were shopping there for supplies. Often London-based regiments sent their Quarter Blokes out for 'a gross of three-inch Mortars and a dozen bananas'.

It was common knowledge that Caledonian Road Market was a German supply depot. The true story behind Hess: he flew here for cut-price black-market underwear for the S.S., but on arrival he chickened out when Churchill told him the price, unconditional surrender. An easy way to go 'on the hooks' was not saluting commissioned ranks. "Ewe har not salutin' the hofficer – ewe har salutin' the King's huniform." Gunner Stover took this as Gospel. At reveille he would wake Lieutenant Budden with a cup of tea, turn, face Budden's uniform hanging on the wall, salute it, and exit. "There's no need to take it that far, Stover," said Budden.

"I can't help it sir – I come from a military family – if I didn't salute that huniform – I feel I was livin' a lie sir."

"But," reasoned Budden, "when no one's looking there's no point."

"Beggin' your pardon sir – but there is! Many a time, when I'm alone, cleanin' up your billet, when I finish, I face your best battle-dress – and I salute it – no one sees me, but deep down I know I'm on my honour, alone with tradition."

"How long have you been in the Army, Stover?"

"Thirty-two years sir."

"Very good," said Budden.

We had 'Saluting Traps'. A crowd of us round a corner smoking would get the tip 'Officer Coming'. We would set off at ten-second intervals and watch as the officer saluted his way to paralysis of the arm.

DIEPPE

On August 18th, 1942, we were learning how to shoot Bren and Vickers machine-guns at Fairbright. The range was on the cliff facing out to sea. Our instructors were from the Brigade of Guards. We stood at ease while a Grenadier Guards Sergeant told us the intricacies of the "Vickers 303 Water-Cooled Machine-Gun. I will first teach yew which is the safe end and which is the naughty end. Next, I will show ew how to load, point and fire the weapon. Following this, I will dismantle the gun and reassemble it. It's not difficult; I have a three-year-old daughter at home who does it in six minutes. Anyone here fired one before?" I had, but I wasn't going to fall into the trap. Never volunteer for *anything* in the army. So the day started. It was worth it just to hear the military repartee. "What's the matter with you man, point the bloody gun at the target, I've seena blind crippled hunchback shoot straighter than that! Don't close yer eyes when you pull the trigger! Remember Mummy wants you to grow up a brave little soldier, doesn't she? You're firing into the ground man! We're supposed to shoot the Germans not bloody worms! Steady, you're snatching the trigger, squeeze it slowly, like a bird's tits. Left-handed are you? Well, I'm sorry we can't have the weapon rebuilt for you, you'll have to learn to be right-handed for the duration." Then, to little Flash Gordon, who got in a hopeless mess trying to load the Bren. "No no son, tell you what, you go and stand behind that tree and say the Lord's Prayer and ask him to tell you to STOP WASTING MY BLOODY TIME!" The day was alive with these sayings.

It all ended badly for me. As we climbed on the three tonner to go back to Billets, Driver Jenkins slammed the tail-board on my right hand. It came up like a balloon and I don't mind saying

I was cross-eyed with agony. They took me to Hastings, to St Helen's Hospital, to have it X-rayed. I had no broken bones. They bandaged the hand up and put my arm in a sling. What a bloody hang-up. I was going on leave the next day.

By now my father had rejoined the army as a captain in the R.A.O.C., and the family were living at Linden House, Orchard Way, Reigate. I arrived home after dark, having had difficulty getting a lift from the station. My mother and father were not given to drinking in pubs, so after dinner I went into the Bell, which stood at the crossroads near our house. Of course this was the day of the raid on Dieppe and its heroic failure. It was in the papers and on the radio. Some of the Battery trucks had been commandeered to pick up some of the survivors at Peacehaven. Lance Bombardier Lees drove one truck and told me of seeing the survivors come home. They were all silent, their faces painted black; they came ashore with hardly a word said; some of the badly wounded had died on the way back. What can anyone say? Anyhow, that evening when I walked into the pub with my hand all in new white bandages I was on to free drinks for the night. An elderly, dignified man came across and said to me, 'Would you care to have a drink with me and my friends?' I said 'Yes', and, seeing it was free, I had a Scotch. After a few words of conversation the elderly man said, 'What was it like, son?'

"What was what like?" I said.

"Oh come on son. No need to be modest."

"Honestly, I don't know what you mean."

The elderly man winked at his friends and nodded approvingly towards me. Then it hit me. Dieppe. Had I been to Dieppe? If I said no, the chance of a lifetime to drink free all night would be thrown away. Yes. I had been to Dieppe, a whisky please, yes, we went in and, Cheers, I was in the last wave, another whisky please, anyhow I crawled towards this pill-box, a brandy then, and . . .

That night my mother put me to bed; for two hours I had been a hero, something I had never been before and would never be again.

116

DETENTION

October 1942. We were alerted for a practice shoot at Senny-bridge Camp in Wales. Burdened down with kit, I decided to hide my rifle in the rafters of the hay-loft. "That's a good idea," said patriotic Edgington. The short of it was several other patriots did the same. And it came to pass, that after we had gone thence, there cometh a Quarter Bloke, and in the good-ness of his heart he did inspect ye hay-loft, and woe, he findeth rifles, and was sore distressed, whereupon he reporteth us to the Major, who on Sept. 14th, 1942, gaveth us fourteen bloody days detention. For some reason all the other 'criminals' were sent to our R.H.Q. at Cuckfield, but I was sent to Preston Bar-racks, Brighton, alone, no escort, Ahhhh, they trusted me. At Brighton station, I tried to thumb a lift; I got one from an A.T.S. girl driving a General's Staff car. She dropped me right outside Preston Barracks. As the car stopped, the sentry came to attention, then *I* got out. I reported to the sergeant I/C Guardroom. "Welcome to Preston Barracks," he said.

"You're welcome to it too," I replied.

"Now," he said, "from now on you keep your mouth shut and your bowels open."

Then he gave me a cup of tea that did both. He stripped me of all kit, leaving essentials like my body. The cell, my God! it must have been built in anticipation of Houdini. Seven foot by six foot, by twenty foot high, stone floor, small window with one iron bar, up near the ceiling, wooden bed in the corner. The door was solid iron, two inches thick, with a small spy-hole for the guard. No light. "You go to sleep when it gets dark, like all the good little birdies do," said the sergeant. "Make yourself comfortable," he said, slamming the cell door. Every day, a visit from the orderly officer, a white consumptive lad who appeared to be training for death. "Got everything you want?" he said. "No, sir, I haven't got a Bentley." I grinned to let him know it was a joke, that I was a cheery soul, and not down-hearted. It wasn't the way he saw it. He pointed to a photo of my girl by my bed. "That will have to go," he said.

"Yes sir, where would you like it to go? I think it would go nice on the piano."

"Put it out of sight."

"But it's my fiancée sir."

"Photographs are *not allowed*." He was starting to dribble.

"What about statues sir?"

He lost his English 'cool'. "Sergeant – put this man under arrest."

"He's already under arrest sir," said Sarge.

"Well give him extra fatigues for being impertinent!"

I planned revenge. I cut my finger-nails. On his next visit I placed them in a cigarette lid.

"What are those?"

"Finger-nails sir."

"Throw them away."

"They are my fiancée's sir."

"Throw them away."

"Very good sir."

The next time he visited I had cut a small lock of my hair, tied a small bow on it and placed it on my bed.

"What's that?"

"A lock of hair sir."

"Throw it away."

"It's my fiancée's sir." etc. etc.

The last one I planned was with an artificial limb, but the officer never visited me again. He was drafted overseas, and killed during an air-raid on Tobruk; a N.A.A.F.I. Tea Urn fell on his head.

My duties were not unpleasant.

1) Reveille 06:00. Make tea for the Guard. Drink lots of tea.
2) Collect blackberries along the railway bank for Sergeants' Mess Tea.
3) In pouring rain, shovel two six-foot-high piles of coke into 'One Uniform Conical Heap'. (A Bad Day.)
4) Commissioned to draw a naked Varga Girl for Guard Room. (A Good Day.)
5) Trip to beach to collect winkles for Sergeants' Mess Tea.
6) Weed Parade Ground by hand. (Bloody Awful Day.)
7) Commissioned to draw Varga Girl for Sergeants' Mess.

(Another Good Day.)

8) Oil all locks and hinges at Preston Barracks, sandpaper door of cell, prime, undercoat, and paint gunmetal black.

9) Drive Major Druce-Bangley to Eastbourne (his driver taken ill with an overdose of whisky) to have it off with his wife in house on seafront.

After fourteen days I was sent back to Hailsham – I arrived to find the whole Battery boarding lorries – yes! "Prepare to move" again! With my kit I jumped into a fifteen hundredweight, making it a sixteen hundredweight.

"Where are we going?"

"I don't know, it's another secret destination," said Sergeant Dawson.

Three hours later, we were back to square one. Bexhill.

"I wish they'd make their fucking minds up," said Sergeant Dawson.

"Look Sarge, they're moving us about to make us look a lot," said Gunner Tome.

"We look a lot," said Dawson, "a lot of cunts."

"Give us a merry song, Sarge," I said, running for cover.

After the war in 1968, I was appearing at the Royal Theatre, Brighton. I took a trip to Preston Barracks. All changed, the Old Guard Room with my cell had gone – everything had changed – except the large parade ground, that was still there; did I really weed it by hand in 1942? We must have all been bloody mad.

DECEMBER 1942 – JANUARY 1943 – EMBARKATION LEAVE

As the monkey-keeper at the Zoo said, when a new trussed-up gorilla arrived, "It was bound to come." We were going overseas. Of course we should have gone yesterday. Everything had to be packed into everything else yesterday. Somewhere great wooden crates appeared yesterday. "Good God," said Edgington yesterday, "they're sending us by parcel post!" The crates were filled, nailed down and stencilled 'This Way Up' at all angles. Vehicles had to be waterproofed. Oh dearie me! This smacked of a beach landing. Everything was camouflaged black and dark green so it couldn't be the desert. All our missing clothing was replaced. We then ran straight down to the town and sold them. One issue was a large vacuum-sealed tin of "Emergency Chocolate", only to be eaten in the event of, say, being surrounded by the Enemy. That night, in bed, surrounded by the Enemy, I ate my Emergency Chocolate.

The news had been broken by the Old Man in the N.A.A.F.I. hut, the dear old N.A.A.F.I. hut. In it we wrote letters home, drank tea, played ping-pong, banged tunes out on the piano, or, when we had no money just sat there to keep warm. It was in this hut that I first heard the voice of Churchill on an old Brown Bakelite Ecko Radio. On the day of the official pronouncement, we were marched in and sat down. Enter Major Chaterjack, "Eyes Front!" Chaterjack acknowledges Battery Sergeant-Major's salute. "At ease Sergeant-Major." At ease it is. "You can all smoke," said Chaterjack, "I'm going to." (Light laughter.) Smilingly, he starts to speak. "You may have been hearing rumours that we were going abroad." (Laughter. Rumours had been non-stop.) "We are, finally, going overseas. It's what we've all been trained for, so, it shouldn't come as a shock." He cut out all unnecessary gas and told us dates and times. A very Scots voice from the back, "Where are we going sir?" "Well, I know it's not Glasgow." (Roar of laughter.) "Embarkation leave will start immediately, married men first . . . they need it." (Laughter.) A voice from the back, "Don't we all." (Loud laughter.) He told us that there would be a farewell dinner dance at the Devonshire Arms. He finished "Good luck to you all."

It was a time of incredible excitement. God knows how we got so much done in so short a time. Men usually only had one active participation in a war during their lifetime. It was about to happen to us. We had problems, for instance the double bass we had knocked off from the De La Warr Pavillion.* It was stolen in anticipation of Al Fildes learning to play it. It had

* I haven't mentioned this before because I've been waiting for the original owner to die

*Picture, taken at the insistence of my father to show the
Milligan family at war, on my embarkation leave*

been noticed that the bass had been lying in the corner of a
backstage room. We measured the size, passed the measurements on to Bombardier Donaldson who had a crate made to
fit. The outside of the crate was stencilled MARK THREE BOFOR
GUN SPARES. One morning after parade we drove to the Pavillion
and hurried in through the back door with the crate. A few
moments later we hurried out with it, nothing had changed
save the weight had increased by One Double Bass. It was

rushed to our work shops, where high speed work was done in stripping the varnish off, staining the wood a deep Black Oak, then revarnishing. It was whilst in the middle of the last mentioned operation that we got our overseas sailing orders, so, not wanting to loose the fruits of our labours, we decided to give the bass to Harry Edgington to take home for his brother Doug who was desperate to learn to play the instrument. Somewhere in the dark of a December evening Harry smuggled the bass aboard a London-bound train, and put it down at his home in St John's Road, Archway. While we were overseas we had a letter saying that Doug had won first prize for the best bass player in London, and had won a Melody Maker medal. Who said crime doesn't pay? Our leaves overlapped. I went straight home to 50 Riseldine Road, Brockley Rise, where my family had returned when my father was posted back to London.

I arrived at Victoria Station during the rush-hour. The crowds were a weird mixture of grey faces carrying early Christmas shopping. I was wearing my new red artillery forage cap, and felt rather conspicuous. I took the crowded tube to London Bridge, and from there a train to Honor Oak Park. The faces of the commuters were tired and pinched. Occasionally one would steal a look at me. I don't know why. To break the boredom I suppose. A man of about fifty, in a dark suit and overcoat, leaned over and said "Would you like a cigarette?" "Thank you," I said, and like a bloody fool smoked it. A bloody fool because, dear reader, I had just gone through three weeks' agony, having given up the habit. As I walked from the station down Riseldine Road a raid was in progress. It was very, very dark, and I had to peer closely at several doors before I arrived at Number 50. The family were about to have dinner in the Anderson Shelter. "Ah son," said my father, in that wonderful welcoming voice he had, "you're just in time for the main course." Holding a torch he showed me down the garden. "Put that bloody light out," said my brother in a mock A.R.P. warden voice. The voice was in the process of breaking, and I swear in speaking that short sentence he went from Middle C to A above the stave. By the light of a hurricane lamp, called

'Storm Saviour Brand', I squeezed next to my mother. They had made the shelter as comfortable as possible, with duck boards and a carpet on top, an oil heater, books, and a battery radio. Mother said grace, then the four of us sat eating luke-warm powdered egg, dehydrated potatoes, Lease Lend carrots and wartime-strength tea. I felt awful. So far I hadn't suffered anything. Seeing the family in these miserable circumstances did raise a lump in my throat, but they seemed cheery enough. "Got a surprise for you son." So saying Father put his hand under the table and produced a bottle of Chateau La Tour 1934. "It's at Shelter temperature," he said. We drank a toast to the future. The next time the family would drink a toast together was to be ten years later.

Mother related how the week previously the whole family had nearly been killed. It was nine at night; Father, wearing aught but Marks and Spencer utility long underwear and tartan slippers, was heavily poised in the kitchen making a cup of tea, strength three. He was awaiting that jet of steam from the kettle that signals the invention of the steam engine. In the lounge, oblivious of the drama in the kitchen, were my mother and brother. This room had been modified into a bedroom-cum-sitting room, double-bed in one corner and the single for my brother in the other. This arrangement made my brother's night manipulations extremely difficult. However, Mother was seated on an elephantine imitation brown moch-ette couch with eased springs, knitting Balaclavas for the lads at the Front. My brother, Desmond, a lad of fourteen, was sit-ting on his bed, looking through his wartime scrap book, read-ing aloud sections on Hitler's promised invasion. A two-thirds slag, one-third coal fire smoked merrily in the grate. Suddenly, an explosion, arranged Luftwaffe. Mother was blown six feet up in the sitting position, then backwards over the couch. My brother was shot up against the wall, reaching ceiling level before returning. The fire was sucked up the chimney, as were mother's C. & A. Mode slippers. The Cheesemans of Lewisham's imitation-velour curtains billowed in and the room was filled with ash. It was all over in a flash. My mother was upside-down behind the couch. My father appeared at the door. "What's happening?" he said. He presented a strange figure, clutching a steaming kettle and smoke-blackened from head to foot. He

My father appeared at the door clutching a kettle.
(Drawn by my brother, who was there at the time)

said "Wait here," went to the back door and shouted "Anybody there?" He then returned and said, "It's all right, he's gone." Despite the activities of German Bombers I was determined to sleep in my old bed. Sheets! Sheer bliss. Lying in bed I realised that the family was finally broken up – the war had made inroads on our peacetime relationship, I was independent, my brother no longer had my company. All was changed. For the better? We'll never know. We had been a very close-knit family, something not many British families were.

The New Cross Palais de Danse was still open. Next night I took Lily Chandler, a girl in whom I had a fifty-one per cent controlling interest, to the Palais. It was a long room with a gallery running around the top. Chicken wire had been stretched below the gallery because of a habit of people throwing things down on the dancers. A five-piece band was blowing its way through the wartime standard tunes. The room was packed with civvies, soldiers, sailors and airmen, with windows closed and blackouts up, the atmosphere was stifling. I spent that evening waltzing, foxtrotting, and chatting up Miss Chandler. I can still see the bobbing heads of the dancers, and the reflected spots from the revolving glass ball above me. Every dance in those days ended with the waltz 'Who's taking you home tonight', and everyone would sing it sotto voce as they glided around. While I was doing this, the last bloody tram was leaving, so I had to walk Miss Chandler back to 45 Revelon Road, Brockley, a matter of two miles. The raid was still on. We walked back through deserted streets; occasionally fragments of A.A. shells would whoshhhh down and splat on the pavements, they do say if you were hit by one of our own A.A. fragments you could have your rates reduced. Lily was wearing black, I think she had a premonition about me. As we approached Malpas Road a stick of three bombs fell about a half mile to our left, but they passed directly overhead and Lily and I lay down against a wall. While we were down there I tried to make love to her. "Don't be a fool," she said. "That was close," she remarked. I'm not sure whether she referred to the bombs or me. I spent some half an hour kissing her good night in the door-way, and tried everything, but she kept saying "Stop it" or, "Don't come the old assing with me." So I walked another two miles back to my house, bent double with pain and sexual frustration.

My week's leave was spent in 'sitting in' with local gig bands, seeing people from the Woolwich Arsenal (where I had worked before the War), drinking, and walking home bent double with sexual frustration from 45 Revelon Road, Brockley.

I arrived back off leave, and, I quote from my diary, "Returned back at billets to find everybody drunk, jolly or partially out of their minds." The knowledge that at last we were going overseas had given the Battery the libertine air of the last day at school. It was impossible to try and sleep. Everyone was hell bent on playing practical jokes. Beds crashed down in the night, buckets of water were fixed over doors, boots were nailed to the floor, there were yells and screams as thunder-flashes exploded under unsuspecting victims' beds. The Battery was in a state of flux, most were on leave, others were about to go, others were on their way back, some couldn't get back, others didn't want to. One night the barracks were full, the next they were empty, God knows who was running us, certainly all the officers were on leave, what one good Fifth Columnist could have wrought at that time doesn't bear thinking about. I remember very well, one rainy night, Harry and I lay in bed, talking, smoking, unable to sleep with excitement.

"Let's go and have a Jam in the N.A.A.F.I."

It seemed a good idea. It was about one in the morning when we got in. For an hour we played. 'These foolish things', 'Room Five Hundred and Four', 'Serenade in Blue', 'Falling Leaves' and the inevitable Blues. In retrospect it wasn't a happy occasion, two young men, away from home, playing sentimental tunes in a pitch black N.A.A.F.I. Oh, yesterday, leave me alone!

Friday, December 18th, 1942: the place? The Devonshire Arms; the occasion? the Farewell Dinner and Dance for D Battery. It was Chaterjack's idea, and I think I'm right in saying that he paid for the whole evening, because I overheard Captain Martin saying to him, "You'll pay for this." For the first time D Battery band didn't play, the music was provided by Jack Shawe and His Band. We would have liked to have played, but Chaterjack insisted that we had the 'night off' for once.

It was a marvellous evening. We all enjoyed the dinner despite the frugal wartime fare. The enthusiasm of the occasion was terrific. In retrospect I don't suppose many of the lads had ever been to a dinner dance on this scale. It was the eve of what for most of us was the greatest adventure of our lives. The moment for the speeches arrived. B.S.M. Poole rapped on the table with a knife handle. "Order please, for the Battery Commander, Major Chaterjack, M.C., D.S.O." We gave the old man a wild round of clapping infiltrated with Cockney witticisms: "Good old Chater", "Hold on I haven't finished me duff", etc., etc. The major was in great form, he'd already been in one war so he knew what it was all about. Taking a swig at his favourite whisky he wiped his mouth with a napkin, and said "Fellow Gunners" (this got a spontaneous cheer). "We are going to war. It's not much to worry about" (at this he got various groans) ". . . at least not this evening." He went on through a fairly predictable speech, war being "long periods of boredom broken by moments of great excitement; during moments of boredom I will order a certain amount of blanco-ing." Here he got great groans and cries of 'not again!' With a gleam in his eye he went on, "Ah, but during the moments of intense excitement I will order a double issue of rum ration. Now a toast, The King." We all stood and drank and mumbled in that usual embarrassed tone Englishmen have on such occasions, 'The King'. Next we had the guest speaker. "Silence please for Captain Arrowsmith." Captain Arrowsmith arose. He was a tough man, in many ways he reminded me of Colonel Custer, in that he was a glory seeker. He was a brave man, and was killed in action in Italy, "Gentlemen" he commenced "The Royal Regiment have an appointment with the Bosche, and as you know, the Royal Regiment always keeps its appointments." The sort of rhetoric got the gunners all patriotic and he got a storm of applause; he made us all feel important. He ended his speech with the toast, "Gentlemen, the Regiment." "The Regiment," we echoed.

127

"What bloody regiment?" said a drunken voice.

The dinner over, the dance got under way, some lads had brought their wives down for the occasion, the local mistresses and girl friends were all present, everyone knew everyone else. I picked up with a W.A.A.F. Corporal, her name was Bette. I forget the surname. I ended up in bed with her, somewhere in Cooden Drive. I always remember a woman looking round the door and saying "Have you got enough blankets," and I replied something like "How dare you enter the King's bedchamber when he's discussing foreign policy." This sudden late affair with Bette flowered rapidly and we did a lot of it in the last dying days prior to Embarkation. Actually, I was glad when we left, I couldn't have kept up this non-stop soldier-all-day – lover-all-night with only cups of tea in between. I was having giddy spells, even lying down. I don't suppose there's anything more exciting than a sudden affair; it is the sort of thing that defeats the weather, and gives you a chance to air your battle dress. When I went overseas, Bette wrote sizzling letters that I auctioned to the Battery lechers.

THE TRAIN JOURNEY (BEXHILL–LIVERPOOL)

The date was January 6th, 1943, the time just before midnight. An army on the march. Weather, pissing down. Standing in a black street, the hammer of the Germans stands silent in full F.S.M.O. With arms aching from typhus, typhoid and tetanus injections, Edgington and I had been detailed to carry a Porridge Container. "Quick march!" Shuffle, shamble, slip, shuffle, scrape. Nearing the station, a voice in the dark: "Anybody remember to turn the gas off?"

"Stop that talking."

"Bollocks!"

"No swearing now Vicar!"

The rain. It seemed to penetrate everything. We reached the station soaked. My porridge-carrying arm was six inches longer. Down the stairs we trooped on to the platform where the train was now not waiting in the station. Permission to

March to Bexhill Station, midnight, January 6th, 1943

smoke. An hour went by. We struck up a quiet chorus of "Why are we waiting?", followed by outbreaks of bleating. At 2.14 a.m. the train arrived. Ironic cheers. All aboard! and the fight for seats got under way. A compartment packed with twelve fully-equipped gunners looks like those mountainous piles of women's clothes at Jumble Sales. Once sat down, you were stuck. If you wanted to put your hand in a pocket, three men in the carriage had to get up. The train started. As it pulled fretfully from the station, I suddenly realised that some of us were being driven to our deaths! Edgington and I in the corridor decided to look for somewhere special to settle. The guard's van! It was empty save for officers' bed-rolls. Just the job. Removing our webbing, we lay like young khaki gods, rampant on a field of kit-bags. The young gods then lit up a couple of Woodbines. We passed the time with our song puns game.

Me: What is the song of the Obstetrician?

Edgington: I don't know.

Me: I'm always on the outside, looking in.

Edgington: Swine. What is the song of the Barren Female Fish?

Me: What?

Edgington: No roes in all the world.

Me: Rotten! What is the song of the man who'd lost his old cigarette-lighter, and found it again?

Edgington: What?

Me: My old flame!

Edgington: Scum. What did Eve sing when she covered her fanny with a fig leaf?

Me: I cover the waterfront!

Edgington: Correct. One point to you.

Me: It's rude to point.

Edgington: Right, one blunt to you. Just a minute, I've suddenly been overrun by a herd of Drunken Peruvian Trombonists on pleasure bent.

Me: Bent pleasure? I like mine straight. Ta raaa.

It was going on for three o'clock. We fell asleep to the iron calypso of the wheels and the raindrop typewriter on the windows. I was awakened at about seven by Harry handing me a mug of tea. I looked out of the window. We were passing, at considerable speed, through black countryside sprinkled with snow. We must be going north, I thought. I ladled out some porridge into our mess tins. It was cold. Only one way to warm it up, eat it. Bombardier Trew of the signal section sauntered in. He had a large set of protruding teeth; but for this feature he would have been ugly. Seeing the luxury we were living in, he said, "You cunning bastards, you know where I slept last night? Sittin' up in the bleedin' Karzy." We tried to soothe him with gifts of cold porridge. Trew said he thought we were going to Scotland.

"Why Scotland?"

"I'll tell you! We're going to make landings in Norway, it's the second front, mate, we'll link up with the Russians!"

"Oh, Christ!" groaned Edgington, "Norway, that's done it."

"Why?"

"I told my family it was Malta."

"What about my family – I told them Bournemouth."

Conversation was cut short by the panicky entrance of Gunner Simms. "Quick, where's the medical officer?"

"Is it the old trouble, darling?" I said, taking his hand.

"Don't piss around, there's been a bloody accident." Two sergeants came running through on the same errand. They returned with the medical officer. Excitement. A gunner in the forward carriage had intentionally shot himself in the leg with a tommy-gun. The weapon was on 'automatic', and had torn a great hole in the man next to him as well. There was blood everywhere. The medical officer did all he could to make them comfortable. There was no morphia. It must have been agony. They both survived, though the innocent party remained lame for life.

January 7th, at 2.45 that afternoon we arrived at Liverpool Station. An ambulance was waiting for the two wounded men. We detrained. Chaos. Non-commissioned officers kept running into each other shouting orders. Captains bounded up and down the platform like spring-heeled Jacks shouting "I say!"

Dawson clobbered Chalky White and self. "You two! See the officers' baggage into the three-tonner." Great! We didn't have to march. Gradually the Battery drained out of the station. We had to wait hours for the lorry. We loaded the officers' kit on, and drove through the black gloomy streets, with its grey

131

wartime people, but it was still all adventure to us.

It was dark when we arrived at the docks, which bore scars of heavy bombing. Towards the New Brighton side of the Mersey, searchlights were dividing the sky. Our ship was H.M.T.L.15, in better days the S.S. *Otranto*. She'd been converted to an armed troopship with A.A. platforms fore and aft. Her gross was about 20,000 tons, I could be a couple of pounds out. Just to cheer us up she was painted black. Loading took all night; there were several other units embarking. We got the officers' bed-rolls into the cargo net, then boarded. A ship's bosun: "What Regiment?" he said, "Artillery? Three decks down, H deck." H deck was just above the water line, the portholes were sealed and blacked out, such a pity, I wanted to see the fishes. Along each side were tables and forms to accommodate twelve men a time.

Fore and aft were ships' lockers with hammocks, strange things that some said we had to sleep in. Ridiculous! Long about ten o'clock. The lads were wandering freely, exploring the ship. Some had dodged ashore and were standing at the dock gate chatting up late birds. It was their last chance. Other more honourable men were furiously writing the last V-mail letter before sailing. I went on the top deck, aft, smoked a cigarette and watched reflections in the dark waters below. So far it had all been fun, but now we were off to the truth. I don't know why, but I started to cry. 11.30! There was to be a demonstration of how to live in a hammock. I arrived in time to see an able-bodied seaman deftly put one up between two hooks, then vault into it without falling out. It looked easy. Nobody wanted to sleep. I worked out we were waiting for the tide. About one o'clock the ship took on an air of departure. Gangways were removed. Hatches covered. Chains rattled. The ship started to vibrate as the engines came to life. Waters swirled. Tugs moved in. Donkey-engines rattled, hawsers were dropped from the bollards, and trailed like dead eels into the oil-tinted Mersey. We were away. Slowly we glided downstream. To the east we could hear the distant cough of Ack-Ack. The time was 1.10 a.m., January 8th, 1943. We were a mile downstream when the first bombs started to fall on the city. Ironically, a rosy glow tinged the sky, Liverpool was on fire. The lads came up on deck to see it. Away we went, further and further into the night, finally drizzle and darkness sent us below. I set about putting up my hammock. It was very easy and I vaulted in like an old salt. No, I didn't fall out. Sorry. In the dark, I smoked a cigarette, and thought . . . We were going to war. Would I survive? Would I be frightened? Could I survive a direct hit at point blank range by a German 88 mm.? Could I really push a bayonet into a man's body – twist it – and pull it out? I mean what would the neighbours say?

JANUARY 1943 – AT SEA

By dawn the regiment were at sea (but then we always had been). Reveille was at 07:00. Sailors wore bells to tell the time. They would shake their wrists, shout "Six bells", swallow cups of hot tar, sing several 'Yo Ho Hos', tie knots in each others appendages and hornpipe the dawn away. Breakfast was at eight o'clock bells. Two men from each table were detailed to collect it from the galley.

Joke of the day.

"Captain, I've brought your breakfast up."

"Serves you right for eating it."

After a breakfast of kippers, anchors, and scurvey, we had roll-call. There had been soul-searching at high level as we were unexpectedly excused boots and allowed plimsolls, at night we were excused plimsolls and allowed feet. The confined air-tight sleeping of 10,000 hairy gunners below-decks had filled the air with a reek of stale cigarettes, sweat, and a taste in the mouth like the inside of a long distance runner's sock. We groped our way through the fog on to the main deck. The day was dove-grey, low cloud, a slight green-grey swell. We gulped in the clean air. During the night several ships had joined the convoy. Two low-slung destroyers were the outriders. Alongside floated serene, silent white seagulls, whose dignity dissolved into shrieking scavengerism at the sight of ship's offal. There was a canteen on the main deck, open from

133

ten till twelve, then three to six, then eight till ten, for the sale of tea, and biscuits that tasted like the off-cuts of hardboard. Harry and I promenaded the decks. From what we could glean, the *Otranto* was a fine ship: perhaps it was, but why did the captain sleep in a lifeboat? Harry and I promenaded the decks. At nine o'clock and a half bells, we heard BBC news over the ship's speakers. The Russians were advancing on all fronts. Where *did* they get the money? Gunner Simms, an amateur astronomer with a compass from a Christmas cracker, had worked out we were going south. Harry and I promenaded the decks knowing full well we were going south. The rest of the day was spent doing nothing except going south. In our wake the sea was a mixture of bubbling turquoise and white. The seagulls stayed with us two days and nights, then suddenly left. Every third day we were to wear boots to stop our feet getting soft. Whereas the days were getting warmer, the weather was deteriorating. (The worst of travelling on the cheap.) The *Otranto*, with capacity loading, was low in the water. She started to do a figure-of-eight roll. The first seasickness started. In the three days since leaving, the convoy got bigger by six ships and two destroyers; these always joined us after dark. Still no news where we were going. Gunner Simms thought we were on the fringe of Biscay. I'd suffered the Bay many times. I knew how bad it could get and get it did. On the night of January 13th, already in heavy seas, we hit a force nine gale. Christ. Seas became mountainous. We listed alarmingly. Furniture broke loose. Crockery shattered on decks. A sliding table broke Sergeant Hendricks's legs. So he was out of it, though, of course, he could fight lying down. Ha! Ha! Seeing a man upright was a thing of the past. I went round saying "What's your angle, man?" At night the hammocks swung like violent pendulums. The top of Gunner Jack Shapiro's came undone. His lovely head hit the floor. He lay there. Was he asleep? Or unconscious *and* asleep? To bring him round we would have to wait till he woke up and became unconscious. With true military gallantry we left him there. On Captain's orders, we all slept in life-jackets. Bloody uncomfortable. You realised what a woman with a forty-two inch bosom felt like

134

sleeping face downwards on her back. (Pardon?)

That night, the storm raging, I fell into a not-too-peaceful sleep. Next day. Oh dear. Men sick everywhere; some managed to get to the toilets, but as the days passed and they weakened they were sick where they stood. I was all right, but I kept having to leap clear. It was my turn to collect breakfast. With two heavy containers I swayed like Blondin over the Niagara. To complicate matters, it was another boot day. Decks were soaking wet. Containers full, I left the galley. The ship tilted. I started to slide at increasing speed towards the red-hot stoves. "Quick," I yelled. "Phone Lloyds of London and insure me against catching fire at sea whilst carrying porridge!" A hairy cook grabbed me just in time. "This could mean promotion for you," I told him. There was food for twelve, but only two takers: Edgington and me. We enjoyed liberal portions of sausages, bacon, bread and butter, tea, jam. Then started all over again. All to the sound of great agonised retching groans. Feeling fine, we tried to bring joy to our less fortunate comrades by saying "Cold greasy tripe and raw eggs!" We had to be quick. Edgington and I promenaded the decks. Harry stopped: "If only I had a tube."

"Why?"

"It's quicker by tube."

With eighty per cent illness we had to take turns on the anti-aircraft guns. The night I was on was a frightening affair. One of the men on Bofor guns forward was washed overboard. Next morning, there was a service in the canteen for him. Poor bastard. The storm never let up. It was only this that prevented U-boat attacks, though I know many a sick-covered wreck who would rather have had calm seas and been torpedoed. A poor green-faced thing asked, "Isn't there *any* bloody cure for seasickness?"

"Yes," I said. "Sit under a tree." I had to be quick.

Gunner Olins had been told deaf people never get sick. He spent the rest of the storm with his fingers in his ears. The ship now, was one big vomit bucket. On the night of the 14th we had passed through the Straits of Gibraltar – into the Mediter-ranean – and gone was the gale – all was calm. The Med????

This threw the speculation book wide open. Bombardier Rossi was taking bets. Malta 6–4, India 20–1, Lybia 6–4 on, Algeria 11–10 on, Bournemouth 100–1. Most of us thought it would be Algeria. As we passed further through the Straits, the sea went calm like a satisfied mistress. Darkness gathered quickly, and lo! across the straits were the glittering lights of all-electric Tangiers! The port rail was crowded. We hadn't seen so many lights since they went out that September in 1939. I thought sadly of blacked-out Britain, but look at the money we were saving! With Doug Kidgell I watched the magic glow of Tangiers.

"Think you could swim to it?"

"Yesss," he said. "It's only about three to five miles." He was a superb swimmer and, for that matter, so was I – (100 metres Champion, Convent of Jesus and Mary, Poona. I could swim any nun off her feet). I told him if we did we'd be sure of ending the war alive. "They'd make us," said Doug, "do time in the nick." "That's right, we'd be saved in the nick of time." We didn't swim to Tangiers that night. Tannoys came to life. "Cigarettes out on deck." It was dark. Harry and I promenaded the decks. The night was warm, clear, starry. The air was like balm. Phosphorus trailed in our wake like undersea glow-worms. We were given permission to sleep up on the top deck, provided no late-night customs were performed at ship's rails. The joy of lying on your back facing a starry sky is something I remember for its sheer simplicity. Not that we weren't living a simple life. Oh no, we were all bloody simple or we wouldn't be in this boat. With the storm behind us, Chaterjack, M.C., D.S.O., tired of throwing empty whisky bottles overboard, decided life was dull. The band was to play for dancing in the Officers' Lounge from 21:30 bells to 23:59. Regarding this, I quote from a letter I had from Chaterjack in March, 1958, in which he recalls the occasion – "Many episodes may well come up during your reminiscences on Friday.* One vivid one to me starts as early as our embarkation at Liverpool: we had been well warned by RHQ that if we were spotted trying to camou-

* The day of the D Battery reunion

136

flage the band instruments amongst the embarkation stores, they would go into the sea. Being fairly efficient soldiers, we embarked the band – camouflaged as I know not what – and there the matter ended for the moment. It ended until we had survived the Bay of Biscay through which the vessel rolled almost over the danger angle, though most people were below decks, beyond caring, slung in hammocks and racked with sea-sickness. Surviving all this, we turned towards Gib., the sun shone, the sea was calm and a band was badly wanted. RHQ asked shamefacedly if we had wangled it on board, we admitted, poker-faced, that we had – all was well, the band played, people struggled on deck, the sun shone and we approached Algiers in full fine fettle."

It was fun rummaging in the hold among Bren carriers and cannons to find a drum kit. "Oh God," said Alf, "my guitar's all packed up for the trip." "Well," I said, "let's unpack it, we can pretend it's Christmas." He hit me. That night we were in great form. It's a great feeling playing Jazz. Most certainly it never started a war. The floor space was limited, and crowded with pump-handle couples. There were service ladies, with a predominance of Queen Alexandra Nursing Sisters – (where were *they* when the decks were strewn with seasick soldiers?). We saw strange gyrations as the ship rolled the dancers into a corner, then rolled them across to the other one. To include 'Cocking of the Legs' we played a reel. Sure enough, they responded like Pavlov's dogs. At the evening's end Major Chaterjack, M.C., D.S.O., thanked the band and passed the hat round for some financial tribute. Mean bastards. We'd have got more if we'd sold the hat. We had to restrain Harry from playing the Warsaw Concerto. Major Chaterjack, M.C., D.S.O., made it up by giving us half a bottle of whisky. Swinging gently in hammocks, we passed the bottle back and forth until we fell into a smiling sleep. It was the best day we'd had at sea. From now on the weather improved. Those who had suffered sickness were now strong enough to lie down without help. The morning after the dance was perfect. Clear sky. No wind. Calm sea. We were dive-bombed. "Tin hats on," boomed the Tannoy. Gun crews were all caught with their pants down.

(There was some kind of medical inspection at the time.) Chaterjack's batman awakened him: "Sir, an Iti plane is bombing us." "Don't worry," said Chaterjack, "he's allowed to," and added, "Did you get his number?" It was an old lumbering three-engined Caproni. We let fly a few rounds at him, it didn't seem fair, like shooting a grandmother. So we just waved him goodbye. After this attack, gun crews became trigger-happy. The sight of a seagull was the signal for thunderous barrages. It had to be stopped. The ship's Captain addressed us over the Tannoy. "Gentlemen, all seagulls in the area are unarmed, can we refrain from shooting at them? Thank you." Edgington had something to say about this. "Seagulls yes, but what about fish?" We were travelling through fish-infested waters, many of them sympathetic to the German cause. "You're right, Colonel," I said. "There should be regular fish-inspections, each being tasted for indentification."

Me: "Sir, this fish tastes like a Gestapo Sergeant."

Edgington: "Right, drown it, at once."

Me: "It's not frightened of water."

Edgington: "Then drown it on land. Poison a hill and make him eat it."

Me: "Yes."

Edgington: "That 'yes' sounds very suspicious."

Me: "Don't worry, it's one of ours."

Edgington: "Good, you can stand by me to rely on you."

Me: "I shall always remember you like that." (Here I point to a coil of greasy rope.)

Edgington: "Ah, I was very poor then but now . . ."

Me: "But now what?"

Edgington: "But now I was very poor then."

We were only twenty-one.

The end of the voyage was nigh. We wanted to get ashore before the equipment was out of date. Over the Tannoy: "Good morning. Colonel Meadows speaking. I'm going to put you all out of your agony." (He was too late for me.) "I can now tell you our destination." (CHEERS) "We are to land at Algiers, as reinforcements for the 1st Army; we will be fighting alongside the Americans, who will be welcomed into this theatre of

138

The 'I think I see them, sir'
Gnr. Neat

The 'Room for one more inside'
[Bdr Fordham

The 'Flash Harry'.
[Gnr. Fowler.

The 'Where's every body gone'
Gnr Flash Gorda

Lt Beauman Smith

Tin hats, as observed on board the Otranto *during anti-aircraft stations*

operations." "So, we're going to an operating theatre," grinned Harry. "We should be docking at 10.30 a.m. tomorrow. From there we will go to a Transit Camp for brief training. We should be in action three weeks from now." (Mixed groans and cheers.) "Good luck to you all." Cries of 'Good Luck Mate'. Algiers? Wasn't that where Charles Boyer once had it off with Hedy Lamar in the Kasbah? Mind you, they got out while the going was good. The rest of the day was spent packing kit. We were issued with an air-mail letter, in which we were allowed to say we'd arrived safe and sound. News which would now make everybody at home happy. From now, all mail was censored. We were no longer allowed to give the number of troops, measurements of guns and ammo returns to the German Embassy in Spain. This, of course, would cut our income down considerably. So there it was, tomorrow North Africa. I wrote the name on a bit of paper, it would come in useful. That evening with the sun setting, we all gathered around Major Chaterjack on the promenade deck and sang old songs. The sea was still, ships were at slow speed, as the sounds of 'You are my sunshine', 'Run Rabbit Run', and 'Drink to me only' were wafted across the waters. It all seemed very nostalgic. It must have struck terror into the breasts of any listening Germans.

ALGIERS

On January 18th, 1943, I wrote in my diary: 'Arrived Algiers at Dawn.' Harry and I got up early to enjoy the sight of Africa at first light. We saw it bathed in a translucent, pre-dawn purple aura. Seagulls had joined us again. A squadron of American Lockheed Lightnings circled above. The coast was like a wine-coloured sliver, all the while coming closer. The visibility grew as the sun mounted the sky; there is no light so full of hope as the dawn; amber, resin, copper lake, brass green. One by one, they shed themselves until the sun rose golden in a white sky. Lovely morning warmth. I closed my eyes and turned my face to the sun. I fell down a hatchway. "Awake!" said Harry down the hole, "for Morning in the Bowl

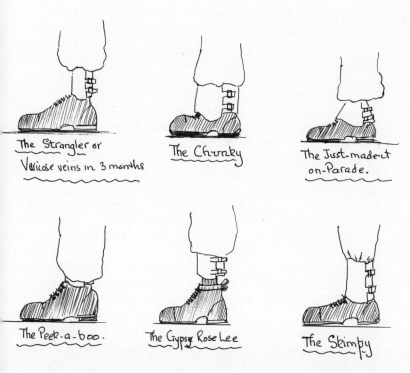

The Strangler or Varicose veins in 3 months

The Chunky

The Just-made-it on-Parade.

The Peek-a-boo.

The Gypsy Rose Lee

The Skimpy

Gaiter styles, spotted on day of disembarkation at Algiers

of Night, Has flung the Stone that puts the Stars to flight. Omar Khayyam." "Get stuffed. Spike Milligan." The convoy was now in line ahead making for the port. Gradually the buildings of Algiers grew close. The city was built on a hill, and tiered, most buildings were white. We were closing to the dockside. Activity. Khaki figures were swarming everywhere. Trucks, tanks, aircraft, guns, shells, all were being off-loaded. Odd gendarmes looked helpless, occasionally blew whistles, pointed at Arabs, then hit them. They'd lost the war and by God they were going to take it out on someone. Now we could see palm tree lined boulevards. We made the last raid on the canteen, stocked up with fags, chocolate and anything. In full F.S.M.O. (pronounced Effessmmmoh) we paraded on deck. I tell you, each man had so much kit it reminded me of that bloody awful Warsaw Concerto. A Bombardier came round and distributed little booklets saying: "Customs and Habits of French North Africa. How to behave. The Currency. Addresses of Post-Brothel Military Clinics." And a contraceptive. Only one? They must be expecting a short war. Harry Edgington was horrified. "Look at this," he said, his lovely face dark with rage, "putting temptation in a man's hands." Whereupon he hurled it overboard. Others blew them up and paddled them ashore shouting "Happy New Year". Down came the gang-planks and the 56th Heavy Regiment, ten days at sea, heavier than it had ever been, debouched.

There were no transports save those to carry kit-bags and luggage. Chalky White and I were lucky again. "You two stay behind. Supervise the loading of all Battery kit-bags on to that three-tonner."

Unloading went on all day. The harbour was glutted with ships unloading war supplies and what occasionally looked suspiciously like Three Piece Suites. Throughout the dusty day the cranes were lifting and dipping, like herons fishing. Our Battery baggage was identified by colour. A blue square with a yellow stripe up the middle. We rode up and down in cargo nets. Puzzled Algerians watched us as we arose from the bowels of the ship singing Ann Zeigler and Webster Booth melodies. Ever present were the Arabs, waiting to nick things, but it was easy to stop them. You hit 'em. It was appalling to see a people so impoverished. They wore rags, they were second-class citizens, they were degraded. It hurt most when you saw the children. I'm bloody glad I wasn't French. Even better, I'm glad I wasn't an Arab. But seriously, folks! By sunset, the job was completed and we were exhausted by a day's hard singing in the nets. Lieutenant Hughes fell us in. We marched through the palm-lined streets, into a vast concrete football stadium. On the pitch were scores of tents. It must have been half-time I thought. But no! They were the bivouacs of a Scots Battalion, just back from the front. Hanging on the washing lines were battle-scarred kilts. It must have been hell under there! It was a vast concrete football stadium. I mention that again in the

142

nature of an encore. All the action was around a field kitchen. Several queues all converged on one point where a cook, with a handle-bar moustache, and of all things a monocle, was doling out. He once had a glass eye that shot out when he sneezed and fell in the porridge so he wore the monocle as a sort of optical condom. He doled out something into my mess tin. "What is it?" I asked. "Irish Stew," he said, "Then", I replied, "Irish Stew in the name of the Law." It was a vast concrete arena. We queued for an hour. When that had passed we queued for blankets. Next, find somewhere to sleep, like a football stadium in North Africa. We dossed down on the terraces. After ship's hammocks it was murder. If only, if *only* I had a grand piano. I could have slept in that. Anything was better than a vast concrete arena. At dawn my frozen body signalled me, arise. I stamped around the freezing terraces to get warm. I lit up a fag and went scrounging. There were still a few embers burning in the field kitchen. I found a tea urn full of dead leaves from which I managed to get a fresh brew. A sentry turned up. "Bleedin' cold, ain't it," he said. "Yes," I replied, and he seemed well pleased with the answer. After all, it was free and unsolicited. I shared the tea with him. "My name's Eric Rushton," he said. "In Civvy Street I'm a porter in Covent Garden." Good, I thought, there's nothing like coming to Algiers to meet a fruit porter called Rushton. Who knows, before sun-up, I might even meet an apprentice gas-fitter's mate called Dick Scroogle from Lewisham. If so, he'd have to hurry as dawn's left hand was already in the sky. A small man in an overcoat drew nigh.

"You're not Dick Scroogle from Lewisham, are you?"

"No," he said, "people keep asking me that." I gave him some tea. It had been a near thing. Gradually the sun came up. There was no way of stopping it. It rose from the east like an iridescent gold Napoleon. It filled the dawn sky with swathes of pink, orange and flame. Breakfast was Bully Beef and hard tack. I washed and shaved under a tap, icy cold, still, it was good for the complexion. "Gunners! Stay lovely for your Commanding Officer with Algerian Football Stadium water!" I stood at the gates watching people in the streets. I made friends with two little French kids on their way to school, a girl and a boy. I gave them two English pennies. In exchange they gave me an empty matchbox, with a camel label on the top. I shall always remember their faces. A gentle voice behind me. "Where the bleedin' 'ell you bin?" It was Jordy Dawson. "Come on, we're off to the docks." And so we were.

Arriving there we checked that all D Battery kit bags were on board our lorries, then drove off. The direction was east along the coast road to Jean Bart. We sat with our legs dangling over the tail-board. Whenever we passed French colonials, some of them gave us to understand that our presence in the dark continent was not wanted by a simple explicative gesture from the waist down. We passed through dusty scrub like countryside with the sea to our left. In little batches we passed Arabs with camels or donkeys, children begging or selling Tangerines and eggs. The cactus fruit was all ripe, pillar-box red. I hadn't seen any since I was a boy in India. The road curved gradually and the land gradient rose slightly and revealed to us a grand view of the Bay of Algiers. Rich blue, with morning sunshine tinselling the waves. Our driver 'Hooter Price' (so called because of a magnificent large nose shaped like a Pennant. When he swam on his back, people shouted 'Sharks') was singing 'I'll be seeing you' as we jostled along the dusty road. It was twenty-six miles to our destination, with the mysterious name "X Camp," situated just half a mile inland at Cap Matifou. X Camp was proving an embarrassment to Army Command. It was built to house German prisoners of war. Somehow we hadn't managed to get any, so, to give it the appearance of being a success, 56 Heavy Regiment were marched in and told that this was, for the time being, "home." When D Battery heard this, it was understandable when roll call was made the first morning:

"Gunner Devine?"

"Ya wol!"

"Gunner Spencer?"

"Ya!"

"Gunner Maunders?"

"Ya wold',"

The march of the Regiment from the ship to Cap Matifou had

144

Dawn of the Burnt Bum Affair

been a mild disaster. It started in good march style, but gradually, softened by two weeks at sea, and in full F.S.M.O., two-thirds of the men gradually fell behind and finally everyone was going it alone at his own pace. A long string of men stretched over twenty-six miles. I quote from Major Chaterjack's recollection of the incident in a letter he wrote to me in 1957. "Perhaps some will remember the landing at Algiers and that ghastly march with full kit, for which we were not prepared. The march ended after dark, somewhere beyond Maison Blanche, and was rather a hard initiation into war – a valuable initiation though, for it made many things thereafter seem easier!" To top it all there was a tragedy – Driver Reed, who flaked out on the march, tried to hop a lift but fell between the lorry and trailer and was squashed to death. The only way to unstick him from the road was by pulling at his webbing straps. Tragedy number two was Gunner Leigh, thirty-six (old for a soldier); as he arrived at the camp he received a telegram telling him his wife and three children had been killed in a raid on Liverpool. He went insane and never spoke again. He is still in a mental home near Menston in Yorkshire.

Sanitary Orderly Liddel was learning the trade of maintenance on the out door hole-in-the-ground latrines. The lime powder that is normally used to 'sprinkle' the pit, had not arrived. He, being of an inventive turn of mind, mixed petrol and diesel and used that. Dawn! Enter an R.S.M. pleasure bent! He squats on pole. Lights pipe, drops match. BOOOOOOOOM! There emerges smoke-blackened figure, trousers down, smouldering shirt tail, singed eyebrows, second degree burns on bum – a sort of English loss of face.

He was our last casualty before we actually went into action. Next time it would be for real.